FORD PICKUP
COLOR HISTORY

Text by Tom Brownell
Photography by Mike Mueller

Motorbooks International
Publishers & Wholesalers

Motorbooks International books are also available at discounts in bulk quantity for industrial or sales-promotional use. For details write to Special Sales Manager at the Publisher's address

Library of Congress Cataloging-in-Publication Data Available

ISBN 0-87938-913-3

On the front cover: One of the special truck models Ford offered in 1970 was the Ranger. This example is owned by Wilber Bergman, Thomasboro, Illinois. It has a 360ci V-8 engine and still has its original paint.

On the back cover: Ford made great strides in styling with its 1940 pickups. The handsome 1940 model is owned by George and Nancy Edwards of North Palm Beach, Florida, and the sharp blue 1950 F1 is owned by Carl and Frank Childs, Boca Raton, Florida.

Printed and bound in Hong Kong

Acknowledgments

The following friends and Ford truck authorities assisted in the writing of this book:
Don Bunn—1948-52
Jay Long—Econoline
Len Kutschman—F-100 Telephone Truck
Gene Makrancy—Ranchero, Durango
Bob Thatcher—1942-47 colors
Ovy Waddoups—The Early Years

Contents

Chapter 1

In the Beginning... 1896-1927

By Robert Waddoups

On June 30, 1863, in Dearborn, Michigan, a man was born of whom Will Rogers later said, "It will take a hundred years to tell whether he helped or hurt us, but he certainly didn't leave us where he found us."

Henry Ford was always fascinated by machinery and constantly tinkered with everything from watches to steam engines to electric dynamos. He became the quintessential enigma of the machine age, and his name still epitomizes both the automobile and the principles of modern mass production begun by Eli Whitney.

On June 4, 1896, Ford completed work on and drove his first car, the Quadracycle. Several days later he became the first driver on record to hit a pedestrian. Over the next three years, Henry obtained enough backing from several sources (including the Daisy BB Gun Company) to start the Detroit Auto Company. He resigned in 1901 because shareholders hired a professional engineer to design the product, and Henry, a high school dropout, felt that he was los-

Hucksters have become popular with Model T collectors because the wooden body (either home built or available as a kit) can be mounted on any Model T car chassis. The only sheet metal needed is the hood, fenders, and running boards.

The question confronting a first-time Model T operator is, "what do I do with three pedals?" Helpfully, Ford marked the function of each with a letter cast into the pedal's face. The "C" on the left pedal stands for Clutch. Pressing this pedal part way down disengaged the transmission gears. Pressing and holding the C pedal all the way down engaged low speed. To travel in this gear, the driver had to continue to apply pressure on the left pedal—leading to boasts among Model T drivers of the strength built up in their left legs. Pressing on the center pedal engaged reverse, while the right pedal operated the brake on the transmission. Panic stops were often made by tromping on all three pedals simultaneously—something that apparently didn't damage the transmission.

ing creative control of the company. Soon after his departure, the company folded.

Two years later, Ford finished work on his first racer. He drove it to victory against Henry Winton. This generated enough interest in the car to enable Ford and a second group of backers to form the Henry Ford Company. Henry left this company when he and the other shareholders argued over whether the next car was to be a production model or, as Ford wanted, another racer. In 1904 Henry Ford finished work on one of his most famous creations—Old 999. He hired a young daredevil by the name of Barney Oldfield to drive the monster to an unprecedented series of victories and land speed records. Again, the interest generated by this automobile brought prospective backers flocking to Ford's door. The result became the Ford Motor Company of today. The first Ford car, the Model A, was assembled by the company from engines, transmissions, and drive axles purchased from the Dodge Brothers Machine Shop for $250 per assembly. The bodies, made by a local carriage company cost $52, while the Hartford Rubber Company provided the tires for $40 a set. The completed Model A was sold for $850.

On March 19, 1915, Henry Ford became one of the most controversial men of the decade when, at the urging of his friend and partner James Couzins, he

A Model T for Christmas
by Bob Surmeier

My 1926 Model T Ford roadster pickup might have been a Christmas present. The original title indicates that it was sold new on December 23, 1926. The first owner was a farmer in Montrose in southern Colorado. He kept it in the barn most of the time, but he would drive it to town on Saturdays to do his shopping. It was sold to the second owner in 1960. That owner ran an auto parts store in Montrose and used it for advertising. When he moved to Boulder, Colorado, a few years later, the Model T came along in the back of a 1966 Chevrolet three-quarter-ton pickup.

When the second owner decided to sell the Model T in 1971, I was not the first one in line with money to buy it, but I was the first to impress the owner that I'd keep it in its original unrestored condition. My Model T still has the original paint—Ford Commercial Green with black fenders—and is still very presentable. The top, seat upholstery, belts, hoses, and tires have all been replaced in recent years because of old age and deterioration. I have also done quite a bit of cleaning and detailing and added a few accessories. However, the little truck has needed very little major mechanical work and runs just like it was built to run some sixty-three years ago.

raised workers' wages to $5 a day and started the Ford Sociological Department to ensure the welfare of his workers and their families. The working class hailed him as a hero and a champion of human rights, while the elite called him a socialist bent on the destruction of the very fabric of American life. Reporters mobbed him, and everyone, including the working class, bought Fords in record numbers.

The first Ford commercial truck was the 1905 Delivery Car. It consisted of a

During the Model T's heyday, numerous after-market bodies were supplied to adapt the "universal car" to a variety of special purposes. One of these bodies, called the Huckster, converted the Model T into a small truck from which its operator could sell fruits and vegetables. Often the rear cargo area was fitted with roll-up canvas screens that could be lowered and snapped in place to protect the vendor's wares from inclement weather or to "close up shop" when the vendor wanted to leave the truck unattended.

No gas pedal, no clutch; what could be easier to drive? Indeed, one of the reasons for the Model T's great appeal was its ease of operation. Those learning to operate a car for the first time didn't have to worry about coordinating their left and right feet to give the car just enough gas while releasing the clutch, because that's not how a Model T was driven. Engine speed was set by pulling down a lever on the steering column, while treadling the pedals on the floor engaged the transmission's three speeds: low, high, and reverse. The 1925 Ford Huckster seen in this and accompanying photos is owned by Daryl Capron of Largo, Florida.

Ford introduced its Model TT one-ton truck in 1917. Although rated at one ton, the TT used the same 176.7ci 20hp engine as Model T cars and pickups, as well as Ford's famous planetary transmission. The frame was stretched a little to provide about the same amount of cargo space as a modern pickup. The Model TT seen here hails from Sealand, The Netherlands, where it was used to deliver potatoes.

Rum Runner
by Alan Hughes

For more than ten years I have owned a one-ton 1922 TT stake body. My son Dave and I performed most of the restoration work on this truck. It was a real basket case when we started, and we restored it with nothing but parts salvaged from other '22s where necessary to keep it all original.

This winter Dave and I rebuilt and installed an electric starter to save this old "pill pusher's" back. (I own a local pharmacy.) The starter was also from a 1922 TT. I have the original bill of sale made out to Lenord Russell of Danvers, Massachusetts, on March 30, 1922. The bill of sale is from the Harper Garage Company of Salem, Mass. The truck had an original price of $649.27, which included a Martin-Perry stake body and a windshield that is listed at $19.50.

As the address on the bill of sale is only twenty-five miles from my home in Andover, we traced down the relatives of the Russell family and met Mr. Russell who is at least 90. In talking to Mr. Russell we learned that the truck was used during Prohibition to distribute whiskey smuggled from Canada. The whiskey was brought into Salem Harbor by fast speed boats from a mother ship off the coast. It was hidden under produce grown on the Russell farm and trucked to a distributor just west of Boston. With this information we have named the truck "Rum Runner."

converted Model C car with a delivery body mounted on its 78 inch (in) wheelbase. This truck was powered by a 10 horsepower (hp), two cylinder, 120.5 cubic inch (ci) engine that drove a two-speed Dodge Brothers transmission that sent power to the rear wheels via chain drive. Ten of these trucks were produced at a cost of $950 each, but the line was

Through 1926, Model Ts used wood spoke wheels with demountable rims. In 1926 and 1927, steel spoke wheels of 21in. diameter were available as a dress-up option. In an era before snow plows, Model T owners living in northern climates usually stored their cars in a carriage barn or shed for the winter. Often this prolonged storage caused the spokes to dry out, causing the wheels to become wobbly and unsafe. A typical "fix" for this problem was to drive the Model T into a shallow stream and let the wood soak up moisture, causing the spokes to swell and restoring the wheels to safe operating condition.

Simplicity is seen under the hood, too. The Model T's four-cylinder engine displaced 176.7ci and produced all of 20hp. Since Ford didn't equip the Model T engine with a water pump, cooling resulted from what Ford literature referred to as the "Thermo-Syphon or Gravity System." What this meant was that the coolant circulated naturally as the hot water rose in the engine block and flowed into the radiator, while cooler water circulated from the bottom of the radiator into the engine. Although this system wasn't very efficient, it did work.

This clever Model T truck display, consisting of a wrecker truck hoisting a home-built Model T pickup, can often be seen at the Antique Truck Club of America's annual Father's Day Weekend meet in Macungie, Pennsylvania. The pickup is constructed in the fashion of many Model T trucks, by cutting off the rear seat section of a touring car and bolting a pickup box in its place. In contrast, Ford built its production pickups by replacing a roadster turtle deck with a pickup box.

shut down at the end of the 1905 model year. The Ford Factory did not produce another commercial truck until 1912. All Ford trucks produced from 1906-1911 were aftermarket conversions of Model C, N, and T cars.

In 1912, the delivery car was reintroduced. This was the result of two years of extensive testing of the body style by the John Wanemaker Stores in New York and through nationwide testing by the Bell Telephone Company. It had the same 1905 body mounted on a Model T chassis and powered by a 22hp, four cylinder, 176.7ci engine through the standard Model T running gear. Ford produced 17,354 of these delivery cars at a cost of $590-$700 each.

The 1912 delivery car remained essentially unchanged until 1925 and was advertised by the company as "The car that delivers the goods. Stronger than an army mule and cheaper than a team of horses."

The next significant change occurred in 1917 when the Model TT (one-ton) truck was introduced. Although this was the first factory one-ton truck, there had been aftermarket conversions available for several years. The Model TT was a beefed-up Model T chassis powered by a 176.7ci, four cylinder, 20hp engine and was one of the first vehicles produced with a dual braking system. This truck cost from $550-$600 and 111,924 were produced.

In 1925, Ford introduced its first pickup truck consisting of a small box mounted in place of the turtle deck on the back of a Model T roadster. Over 137,000 were produced, and the retail price for each was $281. During its last year of production, 1927, the Model T pickup cost $380.

By 1927, even Henry had to concede that the end of the Model T had come. Ford had fallen to number three sales position behind Chevy and Dodge. As the twenties roared to a close, the Ford Motor Company was in serious financial trouble brought on by its continuing to produce and sell an obsolete product for too long. Yet during the thirties, in spite of worldwide financial collapse, the world and the company survived, and the cars and trucks Ford produced in these troubled years would eventually be sought after by generations of collectors.

Restoring a vintage Ford pickup can be a fulfilling and enjoyable task. The vintage truck's mechanics are simple—at least in comparison with today's trucks—and body metal is thick enough to be forgiving in an amateur body man's hands. The truck shown here is undergoing a complete refurbishing at Hibernia Auto Restorations, Inc., in Hibernia, N.J.

Chapter 2

The Model A: Elegance in Simplicity

At the age of 14, I had my own business—mowing lawns for summer cottagers on Lake Ontario. The only problem: I lived about a quarter-mile inland from the lake, so how was I to get the lawn mower (and myself) to my customers' homes and back home when I had finished? At first my Dad did the hauling, but this was inconvenient, for both him and me. Then the idea struck, why not get that abandoned Model A pickup running—the one that had been cut down to a "runabout" for farm use— and let me use it to haul the mowers (driving on farm property, not the highway) to the cottages? I well remember the excitement I felt that August afternoon as my father replaced the well-used and -abused little truck's spark plugs, filed and gapped the points, installed a freshly charged battery, and pressed the starter pedal. A couple of spins while Dad held open the choke, and the engine caught. I can't hear that distinctive Model A engine sound today

With the Model A, Ford offered two styles of pickup trucks: the closed cab and the open, or "roadster" pickup shown here. The open pickup is by far the more popular style with collectors. One of the unusual features of this truck is that the top doesn't fold down—like it does on a roadster car. Instead, the entire top lifts off, enabling the driver to enjoy open-air motoring.

All Model A cars and light trucks used attractive, yet sturdy steel spoke wheels. Although in 1928 and 1929, these wheels were 21in. diameter, the same as the 1926-1927 Model T, Model A and T wheels are different and do not interchange. In 1930, Ford reduced the wheel size to 19in.

without thinking of that blissful afternoon when I acquired driving rights to my first "car."

As everyone with even the faintest knowledge of Fords knows, Model As were (are) tough. The runabout had survived a fit of my uncle's anger that had left a thumb-sized dent in the top of the radiator shell where he had struck it with the crank, and it would suffer untold neglect at the hands of my cousins after I "retired" from my lawn care career to pursue college study. Yet when I retrieved it for restoration years later, the tough-hearted truck would still start and run, though its appetite for oil suggested that the engine was very tired indeed.

My pickup had started life as a 1929 model, or so I thought. By the time I acquired it, the body had been hacksawed off at the cowl, leaving only the pickup designation on the license registration and a side-mounted tire as clues of its identify (all Model A pickups came with a driver's side fender-mounted tire as standard equipment). During all four years of Model A production (1928-1931) Ford offered two basic pickup models: a closed cab and open cab. As might be expected, pickups and larger AA trucks shared the same cab. Henry Ford made it a policy to get as much use out of anything he designed as possible. It should come as no surprise then that 1928-1929

Model A closed cab pickups used doors from 1926-1927 Model T coupes. As trucks they had painted radiator shells and no rear bumpers. The closed cab model also had a metal box attached to the passenger side kick panel for storing invoices, dispatch papers, pencils, or what have you. In almost every other way, a Model A pickup is the same as any Model A Ford car.

The Model A represented as dramatic a departure from the Model T as the incandescent light bulb did from kerosene lighting. Engine horsepower doubled to 40, and a three-speed sliding gear transmission replaced the simple-but-crude planetary transmission of the Model T. Four-wheel mechanical brakes offered sure stopping power and the gas tank, now located on top of the cowl, assured gravity-feed gasoline flow even on the steepest hill.

Elegance, which is sometimes achieved through lavish ornamentation, is more artfully expressed through simplicity. With the Model A, Henry Ford achieved a level mechanical simplicity that qualifies as elegant, and in its subtlety and masterful execution of function is more art than design. Often-cited examples include the carburetor, which is held together by a single bolt; the fuel gauge, which looks into the gasoline tank; and spark plug electrodes made of metal strips, which continue to function as well sixty-plus years later as the day they were installed at the factory.

More Model As exist today than all other cars made in the world at the time combined.

Collector fever, which descended on these cars and trucks in the sixties and seventies, isn't the reason. The fact that more than a million Model As still survive (out of the 4.3 million built) results from the simple fact that Ford designed the Model A to last. Although the engine lacked a balanced crankshaft, pressure oiling, and replaceable shell bearings, it turned slowly enough not to overstress itself. The frame and axles contained the best metallurgy available. Simple buggy-style, transverse spring suspension negotiated farm lanes and rutted coun-

In styling the Model A, Edsel Ford adapted the lines of Ford Motor Company's flagship car, the Lincoln, and in so doing created an extremely handsome vehicle, often referred to as the "baby Lincoln."

17

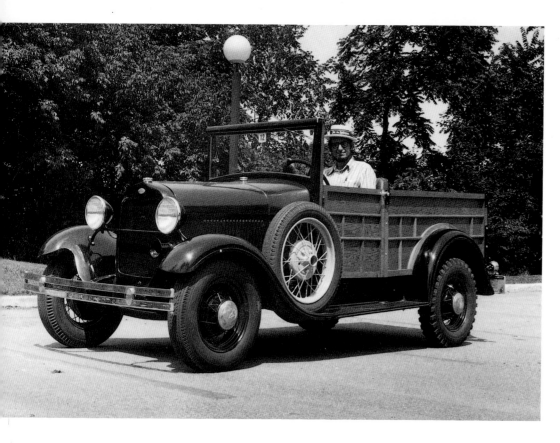

My first car was a 1930 Model A pickup that had its cab cut off at the cowl and the box replaced with a wooden platform. I used this sturdy little hauler to tote mowers for my lawn mowing business. Years later, I dignified my trusty friend with a woody body built from plans published in the October 1950 issue of Mechanix Illustrated. *The magazine honored my woodworking endeavor with their coveted Golden Hammer award.* Tom Brownell

Knowing the warm spot Model As occupy in my heart, my wife Joyce posed by this 1930 pickup during our tour of Greenfield Village in Dearborn, Michigan. In most auto buffs' opinion, Henry Ford achieved perfection in simplicity with his Model A. Tom Brownell

try roads with nary a whimper. Enclosed drive held the rear axle rigidly in place, saving the spring from torque loads. It's tough to kill a Model A. I remember a friend's cabriolet that had such low engine compression that we could count the fan blades as the engine idled, but the car was still running. The fact that almost all Model A parts interchange makes it easy to repair, though the mixture of parts typically found on "original" cars and trucks gives restorers fits.

A Model A pickup's usefulness was limited only by the size of the box, which carried over from the Model T. You could throw a couple bales of hay in the box and still close the tailgate, but you couldn't load in much more. That's the reason my runabout's pickup body and box had been discarded and replaced with a flatbed, making it better suited for farm work where it had to haul twenty or more bushels of apples. My father used to tell of working one summer during the depression as paymaster on a public works road project. When he wasn't calculating the road gang's pay envelopes he ran errands for job superintendent in a 1929 Model A pickup. "I'd make a run to town and come back with a half-dozen shovels," he'd tell me. A pickup in those days served mainly as a delivery vehicle, though many were used by gardeners. In my teenage years I remember the excitement of finding a Model A roadster pickup working in a local cemetery.

Of the two models, the closed and open (roadster) cab, the roadster style is much more attractive. The cloth top doesn't fold, so it either has to be used or removed. (LeBaron Bonney Co. makes a folding top for 1928-1929 Model A roadster pickups that looks original but can be lowered while still attached to the truck.) From a comfort standpoint, the closed cab pickup offered more appeal. The door windows cranked up, the windshield could be opened out for summertime ventilation, and a simple manifold heater kept the cab warm in the winter. On a roadster pickup, side curtains had to be installed to keep out rain and snow. (The curtains stored in a compartment under the seat.) And, as mentioned, once the top had been removed (for summertime use), it couldn't simply be popped back in place if you were caught in a rainstorm away from home. Both style pickups were offered in all four years of

Model A production, but in the 1930 and 1931 series, the roadster pickup is quite scarce. During the 1928-1929 run, roadster pickups seem almost as plentiful as the closed cab models.

Although any Model A is easily recognizable, a substantial styling change separates the 1928-1929 from the 1930-1931 models. The early styling bears a strong resemblance to the 1926-1928 Lincolns and so reflects the artistic taste of Edsel Ford. Distinguishing features of the early Model A include a low, Lincoln-style radiator, sloping cowl, nearly cycle-style front fenders, concave curves at the ends of the front bumper, and screw-on radiator and gasoline caps. The restyle that appeared in 1930 is distinguished by a taller radiator with a nearly straight line across the hood to the cowl, fuller fenders, a mildly convex-shaped front bumper, and twist-on radiator and gasoline caps. Except for the pickup box, none of the sheet metal interchanges between an early 1928-1929 and later 1930-1931 Model A.

Probably the least known, rarest Model A pickup is an early 1930 model that continued the 1929 cab and forward sheet metal. The only feature of the later styling to be found on this truck is the 1930-1931 type twist-on gasoline filler cap. I discovered that this rare carryover pickup existed by owning one. My runabout had a 1930 style twist-on gasoline cap. It was obvious that no one had altered the tank's filler neck, and 1928-1929 and 1930-1931 gasoline tanks don't interchange. I knew of Ford's notoriety or making oddball changes like this but didn't know its significance until I talked to the late Fred Page, who founded Page's Model A Garage in Haverhill, New Hampshire, after retiring as vice president of American Express. Fred loved Model As and at one time had nearly 100 roadsters, sedans, coupes, cabriolets, pickups, and station wagons stored in barns throughout Haverhill and the surrounding countryside. As Fred and I were talking one afternoon, I mentioned the odd 1930-style gas cap on my 1929 runabout. "That truck is an early 1930 model," Fred explained. "I know, I've got one." Fred Page couldn't tell me why Ford had built a few closed cab pickups in 1930 with the earlier sheet metal but with the new type gasoline filler cap (apparently all 1930 roadster pickups got the new body). Most likely

The Model A Driving Experience

If you have ever driven a Model A Ford pickup, it's an experience you'll never forget. If you haven't, it's an experience you owe yourself. You'll feel the tightness of the short wheelbase, you'll be struck with the 360 degree visibility of the roadster pickup, you're sure to remember the distinctive warble of a Model A's exhaust note, and you'll never forget the commanding ooh-gah of the Model A horn.

Starting a Model A is a little tricky for those who haven't strayed far from modern pickups. It's not that the Model A is cluttered with controls; to the contrary, this is a vehicle of simplicity. But the starting routine has a couple of extra steps. You'll insert the key in the ignition and turn it on, but nothing happens yet. Looking down on the steering wheel hub, you'll see two chrome levers, one on the left and one on the right. The lever on the right acts as a manual throttle control (an early cruise control). The left-hand lever advances and retards the spark (something done automatically on modern vehicles). In preparation for starting you should advance the throttle (pull the right-hand lever about a quarter of the way down its quadrant) and retard the spark (push the left lever to the stop at the top of its quadrant). Now you're almost ready to engage the starter. First, though, you'll want to locate the starter pedal—a round button smaller than the size of a quarter located on the floor above and to the left of the accelerator pedal. Now set the emergency brake and disengage the clutch with your left foot. As your right foot reaches for the starter pedal, stretch your right arm across the cab and grab hold of the small silver-colored knob just under the dash (gas tank) in front of the passenger seat. This knob attaches to a lever that operates the choke. A Model A carburetor lacks an accelerator pump, so to start the engine you will need to feed some gas, via the choke, while you are cranking

the engine over with the starter. Now press the starter pedal and pull out on the choke lever (it has about an inch or so of free movement, so don't pull too hard). With a good battery the engine will crank in a lively fashion and should fire almost instantly (Model As are famous for their starting ability). As soon as the engine springs to life, advance the spark (left lever). It may be necessary to feed the engine some more gas by pulling out the choke occasionally until it warms up—or you can enrich the fuel mixture by turning the choke knob clockwise, which connects directly to the carburetor's fuel metering jet. (Model As really are wonderfully simple; when you pressed the starter pedal you pushed a copper jumper against a copper pad on the top of the starter housing. That's as elementary a contact method as there is.) As the engine warms up don't forget to lean the fuel mixture (turn the choke knob counter-clockwise).

To head down the road, select first gear (a Model A uses a standard three-speed H pattern) and let out the clutch. Often you'll feel a slight buck or chatter when you let out the clutch. The rear main bearing oil seal is not very effective and so oil sprays off the bearing and onto the clutch, causing the chatter. As a "fix" for this, Ford drilled a hole in bottom of bell housing for the oil to drain out. Shifts from first to second and from second to third are made leisurely due to straight cut gears. To downshift you must double-clutch with finesse. Steering is quick and direct, the suspension firm yet comfortable and amazingly stable on corners thanks to the transverse springs. A Model A is not fast (45mph is comfortable cruising) but no slower than most pickups into the fifties. The collector fever is starting to bypass these elegantly simple trucks (and cars), so their asking price is actually decreasing. If you haven't experienced Model A ownership, maybe now's the time.

the reason is simply that there were extra production cabs to use up and somebody thought that since they would be sold as 1930 models they ought to have at least one feature of the new styling. Henry Ford hated waste.

Along with a new look, the 1930-1931 models got lower 19in steel spoke wheels, which resulted in lower top speeds but better hill climbing power. A 2in decrease in wheel diameter (1928-1929 Model As used 21in wheels) has the same effect as lowering (raising the numerical ratio) the rear end gearing.

Early 1930 Model As also carried over the 1928-1929 oval instrument cluster. At midyear 1930, Ford adopted a cluster that's more elliptical in shape that also marks the 1931 models. Lots of other progressive changes occurred during the Model A run. On the first Model As, the emergency brake lever is located left of the clutch pedal and locks the rear service brakes when applied. Several states required a separate emergency brake, and by spring of 1928 Ford had engineered a new rear brake setup that required different rear brake drums and

wheels to accommodate the emergency brake shoes. The mechanical brake linkage also had to be revised. You can see this change most easily by noticing the location of the emergency brake lever that moved first to a position ahead of the shift lever and then to the right of the shifter, where it stayed until the end of the Model A run.

Early Model As are easily distinguished by a red steering wheel. In 1929 the same design wheel was molded in black. For 1930-1931 a redesigned black steering wheel with a ribbed outer rim was used. Model A collectors use a multitude of picayune changes like the different steering wheels to fit a car or truck into the production sequence and determine authenticity. Some examples: 1928 roadster pickups (as well as roadsters and phaetons) lacked outside door handles. These were installed on 1929 and later open models. The fuel sediment bowl is cast iron in 1928 and glass from 1929 through 1931. About midyear in 1931, engineers moved the sediment bowl from its location on the firewall to the carburetor. Early Model As used cast iron forgings for fender and running board braces. As a cost-cutting move, stamped steel braces were gradually substituted, completely replacing the cast iron pieces by 1930. Likewise, the Ford logo and part number stampings are found extensively on chassis and mechanical parts of early As but were gradually deleted.

With sales plummeting and the economic calamity of the depression descending, Ford introduced one more pickup model and made some running upgrades to its light trucks. In May 1931 a new, longer, all-steel box replaced the stubby little box carried over from the Model T. Besides greater length, im-

The winged ornament mounted on top of this Model A's radiator is called a Motometer. Those not familiar with cars of the twenties era find this device fascinating. Really, the Motometer is nothing more than a thermometer with its bulb end set into the radiator cab. By looking at the decorative globe on the front of the hood, the driver can "read" the engine's temperature. Needless to say, a temperature gauge inside the car would be more convenient, but the Motometer was far classier. The 1929 Model A roadster pickup presented in this, and accompanying photos is owned by Bill Anderson of Lake Bloomington, Illinois.

provements of the new design included squared corners at the bottom so that crates or boxes could sit flat on the floor, which was now covered with 16-gauge steel for greater durability. This all-metal box required special fenders that are not used on any other model. Regular pickups shared rear fenders with roadsters, coupes, and cabriolets. In August 1931 Ford introduced its first all-steel body: a closed cab pickup with a solid steel top. Previous closed cab pickups had a fabric top supported by a wooden framework. Steel presses did not yet exist to stamp one-piece tops for cars, but the small stamping needed to cover a pickup's roof was well within the presses' capability and made for a more durable vehicle. Steel ribs replaced the wooden top supports, making this truly an all-steel cab.

In 1930 Ford expanded its Model AA truck line with a Service Car—an express-style truck with the sides of the cargo body connected to the rear corners of the cab. In May 1931 a smaller version of the Service Car appeared on the pickup chassis. Even though they were commercial vehicles, the Service Cars carried a bright metal radiator shell, cowl band, headlight buckets, and taillight housings like Model A cars. (On all other commercial models these parts were painted black.) The body construction of the Service Car matched the AA version, which means that the rear cab corners received additional bracing, and the sides of the express body used wooden paneling with an outer steel skin. Unlike the AA Service Car, the light-duty model had a rugged, steel-braced tailgate constructed much like the tailgate on a woody station wagon. Only 293 of these handsome Model A commercial were built.

The Model A's instrument cluster represents simplicity in its most highly refined form. The fuel gauge, located at the top of the cluster, actually provides a window into the gasoline tank—which on the Model A mounts on the top of the cowl. When the tank is filled to the 3/4 level, gasoline can actually be seen sloshing around the fuel level indicator. The ammeter, located at the right, measures generator output—or more likely if the headlights are on, a discharge to the electrical system. The speedometer, located at the bottom of the cluster, records speed and mileage traveled, and also features a trip odometer which reads up to 999 miles. The ignition switch on the left marks an early attempt to make cars theftproof. Ford manufactured this switch as an integral component to a shielded casing which enclosed the ignition cable. If the switch was tampered with, or the cable cut, the car could not be started (apart from "hot wiring" to bypass the ignition circuit). Oddly, this switch had another feature that actually helped make Model As prone to theft. The key could be removed from the switch without shutting off the engine. The light in the center of the cluster provided illumination to the speedometer at night.

Chapter 3

1932-36: Ford Offers a V-8

Henry Ford didn't like being upstaged, and arch-rival Chevrolet had done just that in 1929 with the introduction of its overhead valve six-cylinder engine. For the remainder of the Model A's production run (through early 1932), Ford salesmen (and Henry Ford himself) had to wince a little when reminded that the other low-priced car with the fancy French name had an engine with two more cylinders. Henry Ford was also stubborn. He resisted any hint of upping the power of his engines by switching to overhead valves (too noisy, he maintained). Yet aftermarket overhead valve conversions for Model Ts and Model As could draw so much power from these technologically outdated fours that they became to dirt track racers what Offenhauser engines were to the Indianapolis set. With the new 1932 models, Henry Ford determined not just to do Chevrolet one better—as he had so often in the past. Instead he was determined to lead the industry by offering the first V-8 engine in the low-priced field. Many said it

Throughout the thirties, again largely thanks to Edsel Ford's significant artistic talents and aesthetic sensitivities, Ford led the industry in styling. The beauty of Ford's 1935 and 1936 trucks comes, in large measure, from the graceful, flowing front fenders and heart-shaped grille, closely adapted from the 1933 and 1934 car line.

By adding the accessory Greyhound radiator cap, Joe Quinn of Pompano Beach, Florida, who owns the 1936 Ford pickup shown on these pages, has embellished the front of his truck with the three famous Ford insignias. The springing Greyhound, a popular radiator emblem on Lincolns as well as Fords, represented gracefulness and speed. Below the Greyhound, the V8 emblem spoke of Ford's famous, low-priced, eight-cylinder engine, while the Ford script logo (created by Wills St. Clair with a child's print set) represented a company name recognized world-wide.

couldn't be done, but Ford's engineers and metallurgists figured ways to mass produce a V-8. The engine made a much greater stir among car buyers (the few who could afford a new car in 1932) than it did among prospective truck buyers because Ford wasn't able to produce the engine in sufficient quantity to offer it in trucks until late in the model year. As a result, most 1932 Ford pickups and other commercial models are powered by an improved version of the four-cylinder Model A engine, now called the Model B.

Lack of the V-8, however, did not represent a significant loss to buyers of 1932 Ford trucks. Ring sealing had not yet been worked out by the time the engines entered production and the early flathead V-8s were notorious oil burners. At the same time, the four had been improved with larger main bearing area, better combustion chamber design, and at some point during the 1932 calendar year by a counterbalanced crankshaft, making the Model B four-cylinder engine nearly as much of an improvement over the Model A version as the A had been over the T. In its upgraded form, the Model B four put out 50hp while the new V-8, with twice the number of cylinders, offered only slightly more muscle with a 65hp rating.

If Ford trucks didn't benefit substantially from the new V-8 engine, they certainly shared in the engaging new

From the Model A days through 1934, Ford pickups had mounted the spare tire in the passenger side front fender. In 1935, the spare was repositioned on the side of the bed, a more convenient and less obtrusive location.

One of the most unusual Ford pickups is this Australian "Ute" of 1933 or 1934 vintage. Although at first glance a Ute appears to be a regular roadster pickup, there are some tell-tale differences. First, domestic Ford pickups never used the handsome 1933-1934 passenger car grille (pickups and trucks carried the 1932 "deuce" grille through 1934). Second, the Ute pickup box flows from the body contour (like the Ranchero) rather than being a separate entity as on US-built pickups.

styling. As had been traditional at Ford, trucks of all sizes shared their front-end appearance with the car line. For 1932 this meant a painted, slightly V-shaped radiator grille, larger headlights (Ford continued the practice of painting the headlight buckets on its trucks black), even more gracefully curved fenders that gave the impression of motion even when the truck was standing still, a larger box, and a 10in increase in overall length.

Ford continued to offer pickups in two body styles: open (roadster) and closed cab. Both shared an all-steel bed that looks very similar to the Model A all-steel pickup box that became available in May of 1931, but the 1932 version is longer: 70 1/2in compared with 61in. The all-steel box got its name from the sheet steel flooring with pressed-in skid strips covering a wooden subfloor. Ford would offer steel-over-wood flooring on its pickups into the fifties. The closed-cab pickup had only metal paneling on the insides of the doors while the open pickup had fiberboard door coverings

like those on open passenger cars. Both closed and open pickup bodies mounted on the new 106in passenger car wheelbase.

Contradictory though it sounds, Ford changed the 1933 pickup models by keeping their styling the same as 1932. From 1929 at least, Ford trucks had gotten annual styling changes along with cars. Now Ford determined that its trucks would stand in place for a few years. This saved retooling for new cab stampings at a time when sales were at an all-time low due to the near collapse of the nation's economy. However, Ford's light trucks did receive the longer 112in wheelbase adopted by the car line, which necessitated slight changes in the side stampings of the box. In 1932, the distance from the front of the rear wheel-well to the front vertical molding on the box sides measured 4in. For 1933 this

Maybe the Ford in Your Future Is a *New* 1936 Pickup

Most of us are familiar with what are called repli-cars—cars with classic era styling riding on modern chassis and using late model engines. Now there is a repli-truck, a completely authentic looking 1936 Ford pickup that has been molded in fiberglass by Coachworks of Yesteryear. Why recreate the 1936 Ford pickup you say? Let's look at some reasons.

Anyone who has looked at the new car sales charts knows that light trucks have incredible buyer appeal. And with the popularity of old time styling it makes sense that there would be a market for a new pickup wearing a classic 1936 Ford body. That's exactly what Coachworks of Yesteryear has done with their repli-truck.

In explaining why he chose the 1936 Ford, Chuck Arnone, the repli-truck's creator says, "My love affair with the '36 Ford pickup goes way back to the mid-forties when my Uncle Casper had one on his vegetable farm. If was so much fun to ride on the running boards and tailgate that I loaded lots of lettuce and celery in exchange for the pleasure of riding in that truck. Little did I know that one day I would replicate this neat truck."

Mid-thirties Fords—both cars and trucks—have a timeless styling that looks as clean and fresh today as it did new. But if you've got a 1936 Ford pickup, chances are you're not going to drive it every day. The mechanical brakes are one reason. Not wanting to subject a 55-year-old antique to the rigors of today's traffic is another. Neither of these concerns applies to a repli-truck. Arnone has engineered the stock-dimensioned body to mate to any 1983 to present Ford Ranger 113.9in longbed chassis. (If desired, the fiberglass pickup body and box can also be set up to fit either a stock Ford frame or a reproduction 1935-1940 Ford frame of Arnone's design.)

Combining the 1936 Ford pickup body and modern chassis gives a boulevard ride, Interstate cruising speed, and the reliability of modern mechanical assemblies—with the look of a classic pickup. Coachworks of Yesteryear's new 1936 Ford pickup can be purchased either as a drive-away or in kit form. The kit, which includes the cab, hood, fenders, and complete box, comes with much of the hard work already done. The doors are prehung (saving all the hassle of door alignment) and the bed is preassembled. These repli-trucks aren't just 1936 Ford pickup look-alikes; the fiberglass body parts can be installed on original trucks and the box even has Ford's famous script on the tailgate.

To keep the original look, the stock headlight has been replicated in steel and modified internally to accept either sealed beam or halogen lights. Original Ford interior kits from LeBaron-Bonney can be installed, or the truck can be fitted with a custom interior.

If you've been thinking about a replica project, this repli-truck might just be it. Building a new vehicle is easier than doing a restoration and quality replicas are holding their value. With the prices of classic pickups on the rise, it's logical to think that a well-constructed repli-truck would also be an inflation beater. But most important, it would be a darn fun truck to own and drive.

---

measurement was 9in, caused by moving the wheel well back to match the longer wheelbase. The V-8 engine, now rated at 75hp, was now in full production and the oil consumption problem of the early engines had been for the most part solved. Ford continued to offer its four-cylinder Model B in 1933 and the counterbalanced crankshaft found in all 1933 four-cylinders makes this a smooth, durable engine. Often the 1933 four-cylinder-powered cars and trucks

An unusual accessory, seldom seen on pickup trucks, is the aftermarket "windwing" mounted at the front of this truck's window opening. The small glass pane served to deflect the wind, allowing window-down motoring without a ruffling the driver and passenger's hair.

are called Model Cs, but Ford lists no such model. The C designation came about because many of the cylinder heads on 1933 fours with the counterbalanced crankshaft have a large C embossed on them. If anything, the C stands for "counterbalanced." It is definitely not a model designation. When new, one could tell if a Ford car or truck had the V-8 or four-cylinder engine by the insignia on the hubcaps. On V-8s the hubcap carried a V-8 symbol, while the hubcaps on a truck with a four-cylinder engine were labeled with the Ford name.

Apart from the engine and serial numbers, there is almost no way to tell a 1934 Ford pickup from a 1933. Visible external differences are a chromed front bumper, standard in 1934, new oval emblems with the Ford script on the sides

of the hood, and the V-8 insignia on the hubcaps, top of the grille, and below the hood side emblems. Ford offered only one engine in 1934, the 221ci flathead V-8. The roadster pickup could still be ordered but only 347 were built. A pickup and panel delivery continued to comprise Ford's light-duty offerings.

A canted windshield and more graceful lines to the cab, a V-shaped radiator grille resembling the 1933-1934 Ford cars, and more streamlined front fenders that wrap down to the bumper in the front work together to make the 1935-1936 models among the most handsome of Ford trucks. The interior also received upgrading with cardboard liners on the doors as well as the kick panels. In addition to a cardboard headliner, Ford truck cabs were now fitted with cardboard coverings in the rear corners and around the rear window as well. Since the restyled cab sat farther back on the frame, the wheel well area was again set farther back on the box. This difference is seen in an increase in the distance from the front of the wheel well to the front horizontal moldings on the box side panels. Since the doors now reached down to the running boards, a short metal panel filled the space between the running boards and box ahead of the fenders. The wheelbase on Ford light duty pickup and panel trucks remained 112in and the 85hp V-8 remained the only engine offering.

A trained eye can easily distinguish between 1935 and 1936 Ford trucks because in 1936 the Ford emblem and V-8 insignia are located in front of the hood louvers instead of in the center of the louvers as in 1935. When these trucks were new, the other way to tell the two years apart was by the wheels. In 1935, Ford's light duty trucks used steel spoke wheels whereas the 1936 models were fitted with artillery style wheels.

The big news for 1936 was the introduction of a miniature 136ci V-8 rated at 60hp. This small engine was Ford's answer to buyers seeking greater fuel economy. However, the gain in fuel mileage came at a great sacrifice in performance and not many trucks with V-8 60s (as this engine is called) are to be found. The

Collectors call this fancy steering wheel a "banjo" wheel—a name derived from the slender steel spokes that look like strings on a guitar or banjo.

The three round gauges, symmetrically placed, gave Ford's 1936 trucks an aesthetically pleasing instrument display. As with the Model A's Motometer, in 1936 Ford's temperature gauge still read thermometer-style. Keeping with Henry Ford's concern to make his cars and trucks theft-proof, the ignition switch, barely seen on the right side of the steering column clamp, also locked the steering (as is the case with modern-day cars and trucks). While this feature no-doubt prevented many a Ford owner from having his car or truck stolen, it presents severe difficulty to restorers of thirties and forties Fords today when the ignition key has been lost.

engine, which is about 3/4 scale of the standard 221ci V-8, is extremely cute and makes a great conversation piece.

As the sidebar story found in this chapter recounts, Ford's 1935-1936 pickups seem to have a timeless styling.

The heart-shaped grille, used on 1935 and 1936 Ford trucks, is extremely handsome, and one of the factors in the popularity of these trucks. Because of their similar styling, it takes a trained eye to tell a 1935 Ford pickup from a 1936. The most easily distinguishing feature is the side hood badge, which is located in the middle of the hood in 1935 and the front in 1936, as can be seen here.

Popularly known as the "barrel" grille, the front piece on Ford's 1938-1939 trucks is something that collectors either love or hate— but regardless of preference, the large oval grille serves to make these trucks uniquely distinctive. Roger Thoman owns this example.

Collectors are attracted to panel models for their ability to carry a load of parts to a swap meet or a group of friends to a show. For 1937-1939, Ford offered panel models in all three light-duty weight classes: half-, three-quarter, and one-ton.

Chapter 4

1937-1939: The Barrel-Nosed Trucks

Ford broke a long-standing tradition in 1937 and gave its trucks styling that was distinctive from its car line. Of course, the car grilles on Ford trucks of 1933-1936 were several years out of date by the time they appeared on a truck. Besides the new grille with its horizontal, rather than vertical, bars, 1937 Ford trucks got a redesigned cab with a split windshield. This up-to-date styling feature wouldn't be seen on Chevrolet trucks until 1939. Numerous other, less noticeable changes can also be observed. The louvers on the hood side panels are shorter than the cooling vents of the previous years. The pickup box measures about 4in longer, the tailgate carries a V-8 insignia under the Ford name, and a tube-type hinge supports the tailgate. For the first time, Ford installed safety glass in all windows, not just the windshield, a safety improvement that is hard to detect without careful inspection.

While there's no problem recognizing a 1937 Ford truck by its styling, look at a 1937 half-ton pickup, panel, or stake with the sheet metal peeled off, and the engine serial number is about the only way to tell it's not a 1936 or a 1938 truck. The double-drop X member frame mounts over transverse (buggy style) springs, the wheelbase measures 112in, and engine choices include the legendary flathead V-8, now rated at 85hp,

or Ford's miniature 60hp version of the V-8 engine.

With America beginning to break the iron grip of the Recession, Ford offered its light commercial models in deluxe as well as standard trim. Basically the difference is in the amount of bright metal. A 1937 Ford deluxe pickup or panel is easily recognized by chrome, rather than painted, grille bars, a bright metal windshield frame, and dual horns with chrome plated caps and trumpets. Front and rear chromed bumpers don't mark a deluxe truck, however, as Ford supplied its light-duty trucks with both bumpers as standard equipment for 1937.

This was a year of firsts. Besides the split windshield, panel trucks used a one-piece roof stamping. Presses with the capacity for stretching metal to the dimensions of a panel truck's roof had finally been developed. Ford pickups first received all metal cab roofs in 1931. With an eye toward small contractors and others who needed a car as well as a light truck but couldn't afford both, Ford offered what it called a "pickup coupe." This first—and last (and very seldom seen)—car/truck hybrid matched its name exactly. To create the pickup coupe, assembly line workers simply left off the coupe's trunk lid and stuffed a pickup box (measuring 33in wide by 64in long) into the coupe's trunk. Im-

practicality more than overcame any advantage in versatility, and Ford offered this model for only one year. Besides low sales and production numbers, one of the reasons that pickup coupes are almost never seen today is that the open trunk invited corrosion in the car's rear section.

As had also been the case in 1935 and 1936, the cab interiors of Ford pickups were quite well appointed—for a truck. Textured panels covered the doors and kick panels as well as the shoulder and rear window area, plus the roof. A rubber mat covered the floor. The windshield cranked out for ventilation and full instrumentation (speedometer, fuel gauge, amp meter, oil pressure gauge, and temperature gauge) was arranged in two circular groupings positioned in front of the driver. Of course, truck cabs were still stark in comparison with a car. No sun visor was provided (although they were available as an accessory), and a single wiper cleared the windshield in front of the driver. (To prevent the passenger from having to peer out through a rain-streaked window, a second wiper could be selected from the optional equipment list.) Armrests weren't standard equipment, and the only door lock was on the passenger side.

Although cab styling didn't change, Ford's 1938 and 1939 model trucks are easily identifiable by their oval "horse collar" grille. Another nickname ascribed to these trucks is "barrel nosed."

So distinctive and pronounced is this grille that you either love it or hate it. I happen to find Ford's 1938-1939 trucks handsome, perhaps because my grandfather had a 1938 ton-and-a-half that he took his grandkids for rides in around his farm. Ford also changed the bed of its 1938 trucks from riveted to welded construction and stamped three raised panels into the tailgate with the Ford script and V-8 emblem in the center panel.

To capture a greater share of the light truck sales, in 1938 Ford introduced a line of one-ton trucks built on a 122in chassis and made heavier duty with a more rugged rear axle, semi-elliptic rather than transverse springs, and 17in tires mounted on split rim wheels. Models in the one-ton load class included the express (meaning a heavy-duty pickup), panel, and platform/stake.

While 1937 seemed a year for "firsts," 1938 saw several lasts. This was the last year (until 1951) that Ford offered a "Deluxe equipment package." Also, 1938 was the last year for cable-activated mechanical brakes. Reluctantly, in 1939 Henry Ford bowed to progress and installed hydraulic brakes. Cardboard door panels also last appeared in 1938.

With the horse collar grille carried over, at first glance Ford's 1938 and 1939 trucks seem indistinguishable from one another. But there are differences. All 1938s have a dash-mounted ash tray; 1939s do not. The 1938 Ford pickups carried a rear bumper as standard equipment; in 1939 a rear bumper was optional. The crank handle for the windshield sits in a horizontal position on 1938 Ford trucks; it's in a vertical position on 1939s. A V-8 insignia perches on the top of a '38's grille; it's missing on the 1939. In 1938, the spare tire wore a stainless steel hubcap; this cap is painted black in 1939.

Engines for 1938 were the same as in 1937: an economy 60hp V-8 and the standard 85hp V-8. In midyear 1938, a revised version of the standard engine with 24-stud cylinder heads replaced the earlier 21-stud cylinder head engine. For 1939 an extra-cost 95hp V-8 joined the engine lineup. Ford's pride in its all-V-8 engine lineup is evident in the widespread use of the V-8 insignia, which appears on the tailgate, hub caps, and grille trim (1938 only).

With the tonner models giving Ford a foothold in the upper reaches of the light truck market, 1939 saw the introduction of a new three-quarter-ton series using the same frame and wheelbase as one ton, but with half-ton brakes and 16in wheels. Bodies available in the three-quarter-ton line included the express (pickup), panel, and platform/stake.

Options and accessories for Ford trucks of this era included an oil bath air cleaner, oil filter, oversize tires, heavy-duty clutch, governor, road lamps, sliding rear window, hot air heater, and four-wheel-drive. It's not widely known that Ford pioneered four-wheel-drive in light trucks. Many think that distinction belongs to Willys, or even Chevrolet. But

Light Truck Sales for 1937
1937 Grand Total: 618,249 trucks

Rank	Brand Name	Total Sales	Manufacturer	Main Factory **
1	Ford	189,376	Ford Motor Co.	Dearborn
2	Chevrolet	183,674	General Motors	Flint
3	International	76,174	Int. Harvester	Chicago, IL
4	Dodge	64,098	Chrysler Corp.	Detroit
5	GMC	43,522	General Motors	Pontiac
6	Plymouth	13,709	Chrysler Corp.	Detroit
7	Diamond T	8,118	Diamond T	Chicago, IL
8	White	5,933	White	Cleveland, OH
9	Mack	5,513	Mack	Allentown, PA
10	Studebaker	5,129	Studebaker	South Bend, IN
11	Hudson	4,823	Hudson	Detroit
12	Reo	4,254	Reo	Lansing
13	Federal	2,339	Federal	Detroit
14	Brockway	1,593	Brockway	Cortland, NY
15	Indiana	1,371	White	Marion, IN
16	Stewart	1,148	Stewart	Buffalo, NY
17	Willys	1,122	Willys Overland	Toledo, OH
18	Sterling	311	Sterling	Milwaukee, WI
19	Autocar	218	Autocar	Ardmore, PA
	Misc.*	3,861	Several builders	

** In the State of Michigan unless otherwise noted
* Misc. includes Biederman, Corbitt, Divco, Duplex, Fageol, FWD, Gotfredson, Gramm, Hahn, Hendrickson, Kenworth, Linn, Marmon-Herrington, Moreland, Oshkosh, Schacht, Walker, and Walter

Willys didn't offer four-wheel-drive until after World War II (when the company's identity had been totally reformed by the immense popularity of the military jeep), and Chevrolet didn't build four-wheel-drive pickups until the fifties. Ford, in contrast, first introduced four-wheel-drive on its light duty trucks—and cars—in late 1936. By 1939, four-wheel-drive could be ordered on fifty-six different Ford models.

Ford cars and half-ton trucks didn't come equipped with four-wheel-drive from the factory. Rather, the dealer wrote four-wheel-drive on the customer's order and after the vehicle was built it was shipped to Indianapolis, Indiana, where a company named Marmon-Herrington stripped off the body, removed the engine, transmission, and drivetrain, then proceeded virtually to rebuild the chassis. The frame got lengthened approximately 1 1/2in, and semi-elliptic springs replaced the buggy-style springs that had become nearly a Ford trademark. On conversions done through 1938, hydraulic brakes substituted for Ford's cable brake system, and a modified front cross-member went in for increased front axle clearance. For the front drive axle, Marmon-Herrington used a Ford rear axle adapted with steering knuckles. Both front and rear axles carried 4.44:1 gearing. When the engine went back in, the chassis stood several inches higher than stock. All Marmon-Herrington conversions were fitted with four-speed transmissions. The single-range, in-out transfer case sat aft of the transmission, held in place by a special mount bolted to the frame's X member.

These Marmon-Herrington Fords are tough, rugged, handsome, highly desirable vehicles. They also made history. It was the Army tests of the four-wheel-drive, go-anywhere capabilities in Ford light trucks that led to the development of the jeep. Through 1941, all Marmon-Herrington conversions were done in Indianapolis. Through 1947, all were V-8 powered. In 1948, Ford discontinued four-wheel-drive as an option for its cars. And in 1959, Ford brought four-wheel-drive into its own factories. Ford's experience with four-wheel-drive led to its bidding on contracts to build the World War II jeep. Yes, there were Ford jeeps, but that's a story for another chapter.

1939 FORD C.O.E. Street Rod
by Ric Hall

Rusty and ragged and found in an Oregon farmer's field, this 1939 Ford cabover truck was revived by Bob Drake, owner of Drake Reproductions. A combination of restored stock, new old stock parts (NOS), and Bob's own reproductions, the body on this Ford is now the envy of fellow truck enthusiasts. NOS parts range from the tires to the sun visors. The interior looks just like it did when it rolled off Henry Ford's assembly line for the original owner in 1939.

The NOS grille helps make this the most attractive of Ford's first cabover trucks, in this author's opinion. The 1938 model was Ford's first factory-built COE, starting in May 1938, and the hood and grill are interchangeable from 1938-1947. In stock form, the wheelbase is only 101in, a foot shorter than Ford's passenger cars of the same era (112in). This heavy hauler is finished in Ford Jefferson Blue, including the stock stakesides, and the bed itself is varnished hardwood planks. The wheels and frame are finished in black.

The front suspension is rebuilt stock, and the rest of the running gear is all business. A small-block 289 replaces the original flathead V-8, and a C4 automatic coupled to an Eaton two-speed rear axle help update the truck for use on the highways of today. Air conditioning and a stereo are two more updates the farmer never had.

Bob's truck is well suited for hauling his wares to meets. His 1928-1956 Ford V-8 parts include beauty trim rings, 1932-48 locking gas caps, and 1940 pickup hood ornaments and handles to name a few. Bob's company is Bob Drake Reproductions, Inc., and can be reached at 1899 N.W. Hawthorne Ave., Grants Pass, Oregon 97526.

Chapter 5

1940 and 1941: A Return to Car Styling

From the Model T days through the early V-8s, Ford trucks had shared car styling. Then in 1937, Ford gave its light trucks a distinctive look, intended to reflect the power image of a big truck. For 1940, Ford's light duty trucks again wore front end styling that closely resembled the car line. Closely resembled is the key here, because even though the grille interchanges with a 1940 Ford passenger car, the fenders don't—they're shaped differently at the rear to mate against the straight sides of the pickup cab. Adopting car styling proved to be a clever move because the attractive frontal appearance disguised the fact that from the cab back, Ford's "new" trucks were nearly identical to the 1938-1939 models. Nearly identical, yes, but not totally identical.

Changes to the cab and box on 1940-1941 Ford pickups are subtle, but they're there. Now the cab cowl and roof was a single stamping, eliminating any seam above the windshield. For the first time,

Through the clever adoption of a car-like grille and front fenders, Ford gave its 1940 pickups a new look and created one of its most handsome pre-war trucks. The 1940 pickup shown in this and accompanying photos is owned by George and Nancy Edwards of N. Palm Beach, Florida.

the windshield did not open for ventilation and so the windshield wipers are mounted at the base of the windshield, not on the roof header. Another difference: the rear window is smaller for 1940 and 1941. This change is a bit odd since the smaller window reduced visibility. Although the box on 1940 Ford pickups is a direct carryover from 1939, the tailgate received a slight modification for 1941 with the elimination of the V-8 insignia and consequent centering of the Ford script in the tailgate's center panel. Availability in 1941 of four- and six-cylinder engines was the reason for taking the V-8 insignia off the tailgate as well as the hubcaps and nose trim. Toward the latter part of 1941, the grille centerpiece was painted cream, rather than chromed, in anticipation of wartime material shortages.

Besides sharing car frontal styling, Ford's 1940-1941 light trucks rode a close replica of the passenger car frame. Here, too, there's a slight difference between cars and light trucks. For truck use the frame was stamped from 10-gauge steel, while car frames are made of 11-gauge steel. The frame features the

Sealed beam headlights had become legal in all forty-eight states in 1940 and were standard-equipment on all 1940-1941 Ford cars and trucks. The chrome front bumper also came standard. Among the accessories seen from this angle are the right side windshield wiper, beauty rings for the wheels, bumper guards, grille guard, and bumper wing tips.

Next page
To many, Ford's 1940 and 1941 half-ton trucks are the most handsome that company, or any company, ever built.

double-drop design with arches at both ends and is stiffened by a rugged center X member. Wheelbase on the half-ton models, which included the pickup, panel, and platform/stake, measured 112in. Ford continued to use the buggy-style transverse spring suspension on its half-ton models through 1941.

Someone at Ford liked green. Besides a green imitation leather seat covering, the cardboard headlining, shoulder panels, and kick panels are also green, regardless of body color, which could be seen on all interior metal surfaces. A black rubber floor mat and firewall insulator, as well as black steering column, steering wheel, gearshift lever, and emergency brake handle accented the interior paint scheme. The instruments sat in a rectangular cluster (as in the 1940 standard car). The key switch remained on the steering column support. Another distinctive Ford feature is

the spoon-style accelerator pedal with its adjacent foot rest. A sporty two-spoke steering wheel topped the steering column.

Ford's medium-sized three-quarter- and one-ton trucks differed in several respects from the light-duty half-ton models (which Ford called "commercial cars"). These heavier duty models shared the more rugged-looking grille and separate headlights of the larger trucks and rode on semi-elliptical springs with a ladder-type frame. The three-quarter- and one-ton trucks had a longer 122in wheelbase and a more rugged "full-floating" rear axle. The one-ton models also had larger-capacity brakes and bigger tires. These were sturdy trucks. The one-ton express (as pickups over a half-ton were called) had a GVW (gross vehicle weight) rating of 6400lb and an extra-large box with a hardwood floor and steel skid strips, as well as reinforced front and side panels for heavy loads.

The 85hp 221ci V-8 served as the standard engine for 1940 and 1941. The 95hp 239ci V-8 could be found on half-ton commercials but is rarely seen as it was a special-order-only engine.

To many vintage pickup admirers, Ford's 1940 and 1941 models win the styling crown. Giving its light trucks an appearance upgrade by applying the 1940 car frontal styling proved to be a clever move because it enabled Ford to advertise its pickups as "new" when in fact the cab and box carried over almost without change. Elliott Kahn

A much-improved 60hp 136ci V-8 was a third option. Improvements to the pint-sized V-8 consisted of: hardened valve seat inserts; a larger diameter crankshaft; a semicentrifugal "Long"-type clutch, as was used with the 85 and 95hp engines; a revised crankcase breathing system; and an oil filler pipe routed through the intake manifold rather than behind the left cylinder head. Cute as the 60hp V-8 is, it has the power of about a dozen mice and really doesn't belong trying to pull a truck, so it attracted few buyers. Consequently, a 60hp-powered 1940 Ford pickup is even rarer than a 1941 Ford pickup with a four- or six-cylinder engine. All Ford light- and medium-duty trucks through one-ton used a floor shift three-speed transmission, although a four-speed was available as an option on the three-quar-

Seen from this perspective, the 1940 Ford pickup is a study in balance and artistic design.

Accessories visible at the rear of this truck include a right-side taillamp and rear chromed bumper, which is similar, but not identical to the front bumper. Ford did not equip its pickups with whitewall tires, though they could be installed by the owner.

ter- and one-tons. The 60hp engine used a special 3/4-scale three-speed transmission.

Appearance differences between 1940 and 1941 Ford "commercial cars" (as the half-ton models were called) are minimal. Ford nameplates (without the V-8 insignia) were added to each side of the hood, and the chrome molding on the front of the hood was substantially widened. Other detail differences between the two years include replacement of the diecast nameplate in the center of the dash with a stamped plate on which the Ford script is indented, and using square-headed rather than oval bumper bolts and convex rather than flat parking light lenses.

The biggest difference between 1940 and 1941 Ford commercials is in the engine lineup. The 85hp remained the standard engine, but in May 1941 its hp rating was increased to 90 with no change in displacement. The 95hp V-8 remained the same and continued to be available on a special order basis. At the end of 1940, Ford replaced the 60hp V-8 with the engine from its new 9N tractor. While this 119.7ci Flathead four, with its 30hp rating, worked fine in Ford's small tractors, it was certainly underpowered for use in a trucks—and yet it was available in both light- and medium-duty models up to and including one-ton. Any-

221 V-8, yet produced more torque (180lb-ft at 1200rpm, compared with the V-8's 150lb-ft at 2200rpm), making it a much better engine for truck use. The six-cylinder engine's length caused some major problems for Ford engineers who had worked only with V-8s since 1934, and only V-8s and fours before that. Since the chassis had been designed for the shorter V-8 engine, it took considerable ingenuity to cram the six into the engine compartment. To do so, a new front cross-member with a deeper drop had to be designed. Extensions were added to the frame horns to move the radiator farther forward. This required repositioning the hood latch and releasing mechanism as well as extra bracing to stabilize front fenders. Because the six placed the starter on the opposite side of the engine from the V-8, the battery box moved to the driver's side.

The driver's side running board is the same for all 1940 and 1941 half-tons, but the passenger-side running board differs between the platform bodied models, where it is a mirror image of the left side, and pickups, where the right running boards have an extra reinforcement under the spare tire. Rear fenders are the same on all Ford pickups, 1938-1941.

Pinstriping on 1940 and 1941 commercials was either Vermilion Red or Tacoma Cream, depending on body color. The stripe, which is rather wide (nearly 1/4in), begins at the front of the hood molding. As it nears the end of the hood it widens to 1/2in before breaking into two stripes at the cowl, then following the double-beaded molding across the door. The indented section in the door molding is painted the same color as the stripe. The double stripe continues across the back of the cab. Although the standard color scheme called for the fenders to be painted body color, black fenders were a popular, extra cost feature.

Sealed beam headlights had become legal in all forty-eight states in 1940 and are a standard-equipment item on all 1940-1941 Ford cars and trucks. The chrome front bumper also came standard. Accessories for these trucks include a right side windshield wiper, beauty rings for the wheels, bumper guards, grille guard, bumper wing tips, a right-side tail lamp, rear chromed bumper (which is similar, but not identical to the front bumper), an engine oil fil-

Although Ford used the same basic pickup cab from 1937 through 1946, several changes to the interior occurred with the 1940 models. Most visible are the rectangular instrument cluster (replacing the two circular gauges) and the steel covering on the doors (in contrast to the fiberboard door covering used through 1939). A more subtle change, in 1940, for the first time, the windshield could not be cranked open for ventilation. (Notice the absence of a windshield crank on the top of the dash.)

one ordering this engine had to be a fuel economy fanatic. The four used the V-8-style front-mounted distributor with the coil on top and had an up-draft carburetor. For truck use, Ford engineers deleted the governor and added a fuel pump.

An even rarer engine in 1941 Ford trucks is the 226ci six, which did not become available until the spring. This engine developed 90hp, the same as the

By mounting the headlights in the fenders, Ford's 1940 pickups took on a modern, refined look. The styling leadership seen in Ford cars and trucks of the thirties and early forties lay with the artistic talents of Edsel Ford.

Decorative trim on both Ford cars and trucks, such as this hubcap, reflected the influence of an immensely popular artistic movement called Art Deco. On this hubcap, the Art Deco influence can be seen in the boldness and simplicity of the V8 emblem and the equally simple, but prominent stripes created inside the wide arm of the V and the hubcap's circular ribbing.

ter, locking gas cap, low-geared three-speed or four-speed transmission, high-output generator, inside rearview mirror, a heater, inside sun visors, a sliding rear window, and a crank-out windshield (which required roof-mounted windshield wipers).

Probably the most desirable Ford-approved accessories are a Columbia overdrive rear end (which was available on trucks as well as cars) and the famous Marmon-Herrington four-wheel-drive conversion, which could also be ordered on panel trucks and station wagons.

To many, Ford's 1940 and 1941 half-ton trucks are the most handsome that company or any company ever built.

For 1940, Ford's L-head V-8 produced 85 hp. Due to a design characteristic that passed hot exhaust gases over the water coolant passages, Ford used two water pumps (hence the twin radiator hoses running to the engine) in an attempt to keep the engine from overheating.

Some Ford authorities claim that the dual water pumps themselves contribute to the overheating problem by circulating the coolant too rapidly through the engine. Note the generator's mounting position between and above the cylinder banks.

Chapter 6

1942-1947: War Era Trucks, Including Jeeps

Ford built very few of its dramatically reworked 1942 trucks. With the December 7, 1941, attack on Pearl Harbor and America's immediate entry into World War II, civilian car and truck production came to a halt in February 1942. Yet in spite of the short production run, 1942 is an important model year for Ford light-duty trucks whose changes went far deeper than just reworked styling.

The half-ton series received an all-new, big truck-type ladder frame, which, along with a blunted front and waterfall grille like the heavy trucks, moved the half-ton series away from a vehicle based on and looking like a passenger car. The new parallel ladder-type frame with its four husky cross-members now measured the standardized 34in in width to accept special bodies. Along with the frame, the suspension and driveline were also all new. Gone were the former transverse leaf springs, radius rods, and torque tube, these being re-

The gas tank on a military jeep is found under the driver's seat and is accessed by lifting the seat cushion.

Unquestionably the most famous vehicle of World War II, the jeep served in all theaters of operation, from the Russian front to North Africa and from France to Okinawa. No other vehicle was so loved, both by its own troops, as well as those of the enemy. When the German army launched its daring offensive into the Ardennes forest, late in 1944, advance Wehrmacht soldiers cut through Allied lines in captured jeeps.

placed by semi-elliptic leaf springs, mounted longitudinally at each wheel, and a Hotchkiss drive. With the new chassis, wheelbase length stretched from 112in to 114in.

The cab carried over essentially without change, but all sheet metal from the cowl forward was new. The rather squared-off hood front accentuated by a series of vertical grille bars can be best described as ruggedly handsome. The headlights were now mounted inboard of the fenders, with small round parking lights marking the more traditional headlight position in the fronts or the fenders. The sides of the hood carried the Ford name in its famous Ford script. The possibility of seeing a 1942 model with these Ford script nameplates intact is very rare as the top horizontal line of the F is usually broken off. One Ford truck enthusiast who specializes in trucks of this era reports he has *never* seen a 1942 model truck with complete hood side scripts!

At a quick glance, one might think that the 1940-1941 and 1942-1947 Ford pickups are the same from the cab back, but this isn't the case. Part of this deception results from the box side panels being carried over from previous years; however, the box measures 3in wider on the 1942 and later models, and the rear fenders, though appearing the same back to 1938, are also different due to

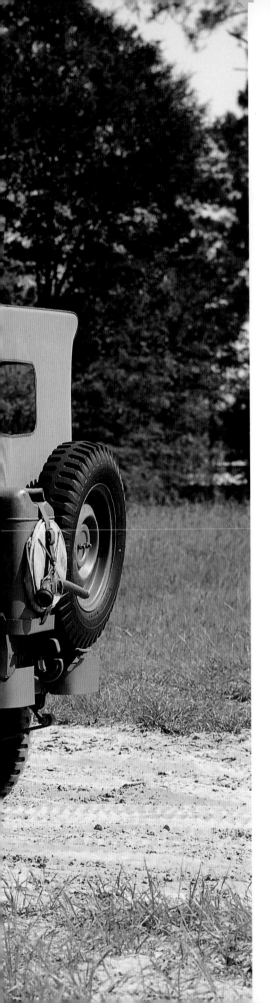

Military vehicle owners take great care to replicate the official markings. On a jeep, these consisted of numbers on the passenger side of the front bumper, a star painted on the hood, the letters "U.S.A" and ID number on both sides of the hood, a smaller star on the vehicle's rear flank, and a star or ID marking on the rear.

Characteristic of military, as opposed to civilian, jeep is the mounting hardware and indents stamped into the driver's entry cutout used to attach a shovel and ax—two primitive, yet helpful tools for clearing a passage way through brush or digging out a stuck vehicle.

the wider bed. Wheels are painted black for 1942, and the front bumper, which had formerly been chromed, is also black.

This was the last year for a Ford three-quarter ton truck until the all new "Bonus-Built" models of 1948. The three-quarter ton models were fitted with 16in wheels with an unusual hubcap that is similar to those used on 1939 Deluxe passenger cars, but with a Ford script rather than the V-8 symbol used on the passenger cars. These caps are very rare.

The three-quarter-and one-ton express pickup box added about 1in of inside length, giving about 3 1/3 additional cubic feet of cargo space. The spare tire, which was listed as an extra cost option, mounted on the right side running board. The three-quarter-and one-ton platform and stake bodies carried over unchanged. These bodies measured 7 1/2ft (90in) in length. Ford built the plat-

form bodies for its light- and medium-duty trucks using the same bridge-type steel construction found on the heavy-duty stake models. The three-quarter- and one-ton series included panel models that also carried over without change except for new sheet metal from the cowl forward.

Engines available in the half-, three-quarter-, and one-ton models included the economy four, the new high-torque L-head six, and the familiar 85 as well as 95hp V-8s. Ford Flathead V-8s are notorious for overheating problems, and during the years this engine was built (1932-1953), a number of methods were tried to improve cooling. To this end, in 1942 the fan was moved up on the engine and located at the center of the radiator. The new fan location required the generator to be repositioned while the distributor received a flatter profile and the coil was mounted so it was separated from the distributor. Trucks equipped

All World War II military jeeps were fitted with non-directional tread, 6:00x16 tires. The jeep's most famous feature is its front and rear drive axles, providing its legendary go-anywhere footing.

with the four-cylinder engine also had a four-speed transmission. The six and V-8s came standard with a three-speed.

A standard equipment truck came with front shocks, a cowl ventilator, 19gal fuel tank, spare wheel carrier, painted front bumper, jack, and tool kit. The extra cost equipment list included rear shocks, hot water heater, right-hand wiper, dual taillamps, a sliding rear window, screen duck-covered seats, oil bath air cleaner, a heavy-duty three-speed or four-speed transmission, and Marmon-Herrington four-wheel-drive.

As war production got underway, copper and other strategic metals became unavailable for civilian automotive use. Accordingly, headlamp bezels, parking lamp bezels, and outside door handles, which were made of stainless steel on early 1942 models, are stamped steel and painted cream on the later 1942 production. The chromed Ford script nameplate on the dash of 1942 trucks (a carryover from 1941) also became a steel stamping, which was painted cream ear-

In 1942, Ford returned to using a common styling on its light- and medium-duty trucks. Along with the distinctive "waterfall" grille, the 1942 and early postwar models used a all-new truck-style rather than car-based frame that eliminated the famous Ford transverse leaf springs.

ly in 1942; it was discontinued altogether toward the end of 1942 production. Besides using cream as a contrast color for these trim items, Ford also made cream the pinstripe color on all trucks, regardless of body shade. On this year only pinstripes outlined the side hood openings.

1945-1947 Ford Trucks

The American auto industry emerged from World War II facing the biggest seller's market the world had ever seen. Manufacturers had been allowed to build a limited number of one-and-a-half ton medium-duty trucks in April 1944 for high-priority civilian users. However, it wasn't until May 1945, with the end of the war in sight, that light-duty trucks intended for public purchase began to travel down the assembly lines. With the huge pent-up demand for new trucks, and buyers with money in their pockets, Ford wasted no time converting its truck assembly plants to civilian production.

It takes a trained eye to pick out a 1945 Ford truck from a 1942 model. Visible changes include the elimination of pinstripes, the Ford script stamped into the sides of the hood (replacing the fragile nameplate), and adjustable rear view mirror brackets in place of the former forged and fixed-length brackets. The early production consisted of half-ton pickups, one-and-a-half ton chassis-cabs

1942-1947 Ford Truck and Commercial Car Colors
by Bob Thatcher

For 1942, Ford trucks and commercial cars (sedan deliveries) were offered in any Ford super deluxe passenger car color, plus Vermilion, a bright red. The colors included Newcastle Gray (a light shade), Fathom Blue (very dark), Moselle Maroon, Niles Blue Green (just what the name implies), and Florentine Blue (a baby blue).

The postwar colors are a slightly different story. The US Government gave manufacturers permission in 1944 to make a few 1 1/2-ton chassis and cabs to help alleviate the truck shortage. All Ford 1944 trucks were painted Phoebe Gray Metallic, which was an exclusive 1942 Mercury color.

When 1945 rolled around, manufacturers were allowed to make half-ton pickups also. Most of these were painted another exclusive 1942 Mercury color, Village Green, and a very few were painted Phoebe Gray. The main difference between these low-volume trucks and the trucks built in 1942 was the Ford logo stamped in the side of the hood instead of the diecast script logo.

By 1946 Ford must have used up the extra paint they had leftover from 1942 because Greenfield Green, another exclusive Mercury color was used on probably 90 percent of the trucks until the end of the 1947 model run. The other two colors are the old standbys, Vermilion and Black.

Village Green and Greenfield Green are very similar colors and you can hardly tell them apart. Unlike on prewar vehicles, there was not much special painting done in the first few years after the war. With the fantastic sellers' market, the program was, "Here's your new dark green pickup. If you want gray, sorry, we will sell your truck to the next order in the book." Those were the "salad" days.

Paint colors for 1946 and 1947 were Greenfield Green, Medium Luster Black, Light Moonstone Gray, Vermilion Red, and Modern Blue. Wheels from 1942-1947 were painted black.

The grille and stripe colors were all Tacoma Cream from 1942 to the end of the 1947 truck model run. Ford was probably inclined to stick with dark colors because the contrast was nice.

and stakes, and school bus chassis. A steel shortage led to the emphasis on cab and chassis models. For this reason production of panel models didn't resume until late 1945.

Every Ford and Willys jeep built after August 1, 1942, came equipped with a "jerrican" strapped to the rear of the vehicle. Often, the additional fuel supply provided by this 5gal container supplied the reserve needed to reach the next fuel depot.

Ford had benefited greatly from building thousands of trucks during World War II. Many of the engineering refinements that had been developed for war trucks found their way into postwar

Ford-built jeeps used four-cylinder tractor engines that had a greater reputation for failure than the "Go-Devil" engine in their Willys-built counterpart. Authorities on World War II jeeps warn would-be purchasers or restorers of Ford-built GPW jeeps to carefully inspect the engine for cracks as replacement blocks are exceedingly hard to find. Note the remote carburetor air cleaner, needed to provide a low hood profile.

The headlights on most World War II military jeeps are mounted upside down on hinges that allow the lights to be flipped up to a position where they shine toward the engine compartment.

production. Ford touted its 1945 models as having "32 Basic Advancements." The most important of these came in the form of a 100hp V-8 engine. Introduced in mid-1945, Ford called this engine the Model 59. Its displacement remained at 239ci, but aluminum pistons with four rings improved oil control, and silver al-

The immaculately restored 1943 Ford jeep shown in this and accompanying photos belongs to Joseph Lorentzson of Jacksonville, Florida. Military vehicle collectors often like to complete their displays with helmets and other items that a soldier might have stowed in his jeep.

loy rod bearings gave two-and-a-half to three times longer engine life. Other refinements of the Model 59 included a pressurized cooling system, larger capacity oil pump, stronger piston pins, and a vastly improved moisture-resistant ignition system.

Not all the "32 Basic Advancements" applied to the V-8 engine. Eleven involved the chassis. Among these are a four-speed transmission, now standard for the tonner, with an internal spring reverse lock that eliminated the reverse latch on the shift lever; an additional crossmember at the rear of the cab for greater stability; and cab door window glass mounted in metal frames to prevent breakage. Both the four cylinder, and the 221ci V-8 engines were discon-

An attractive "speed steak" hubcap dressed up Ford's 1945-1947 pickups. Otherwise, these early post war trucks differed very little from the restyled 1942 models.

tinued. Ford salesmen were instructed to sell sixes in light-duty trucks in order for the factory to meet the demand for V-8s in heavy trucks.

Half- and one-ton panels were added to the 1946 model lineup as the steel supply increased. All Light Duty models (Ford advertising no longer called them "Commercial Cars") were fitted with new 1946 passenger car type hub caps as they became available.

1947 Ford Trucks

Changes for 1947 were minimal as all Ford's engineering and design resources focused on creating the "Bonus-Built" models to be introduced in 1948. Distinguishing differences of the 1947 models are few in number. Carriage bolts could be seen holding the running boards in place. Previously, the bolts fit into a cage underneath the running board and were not exposed from the top. The wiring harness now attached to the firewall with push-in clips rather than being held with sheet metal fasteners screwed into the firewall.

As an interim model, 1942-1947 Ford pickups are often overlooked, but they are handsome, hardworking trucks that warrant collector attention.

Ford and the War Jeep

As a former military man, Marmon-Herrington President Colonel Arthur Herrington was well aware of the Army's need for a light reconnaissance-type vehicle. In early 1937 when Marmon-Herrington began converting Ford half-ton pickups to four-wheel-drive, Col. Herrington offered the Army a half-ton Ford 4x4 as a test vehicle. Drivers showed their approval by calling it "Darling." The Army liked the go-anywhere pickup so well that they ordered sixty-four more for testing. The Ford 4x4s were great for climbing hills, churning through mud, and for pulling loads cross-country, but the Army wanted something smaller, more rugged, and more maneuverable.

Thinking small, the Army arranged to have American Bantam Company of Butler, Pennsylvania, loan two of its cars

For 1942-1947, Ford mounted the spare tire on the driver's side, leaving the passenger side uncluttered to aid in lifting items out the pickup box for curbside unloading.

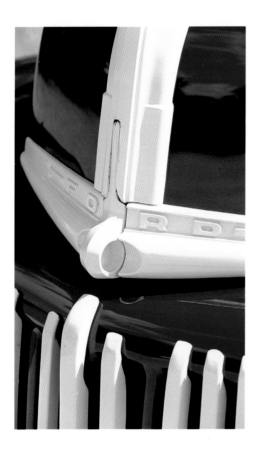

Another small, but noticeable, difference between Ford's 1942 and early post-war pickups is seen on the color of the Ford nameplate at the front of the hood. For 1942 only, the area around the letters is color-contrasted in black, enabling the Ford name to stand out. For 1945-1947, the entire nose piece is painted cream, as shown here.

for testing. The American Bantam was the smallest production car available at the time and small may be the wrong word. Powered by a 50ci engine rated at 22hp with a 75in wheelbase and weighing only 1,200lb, these cars were *tiny*. The Army tested the two little American Bantams on a cross-country course, driving up hills and through ditches with two men cramped into each car. It was immediately apparent that the Bantams were not satisfactory for the job, either. They weren't tough enough, powerful enough, big enough, and did not have four-wheel-drive. But the design for the needed vehicle was jelling.

With war clouds gathering in Europe, the Army Utility Vehicle Technical Committee drew up a set of proposed specifications for the ideal go-anywhere reconnaissance vehicle. In June of 1940

the committee recommended that seventy vehicles built to its specifications be obtained for testing, and it sent a bid request to 135 US automobile manufacturers and suppliers. Only two companies took the bid request seriously: American Bantam and Willys; Ford would respond later. The Bantam pilot model was an overwhelming success. It did all the Army wanted it to. It climbed hills, ran cross-country, went through mud, and so on. There was only one problem. It weighed 2,030lb and the Army's specifications called for 1,300lb maximum. Willys Chief Engineer Barney Roos built his prototype within the height, length, and track parameters of the bid specifications and let the weight fall where structural integrity determined. Ford's pilot, likewise, was overweight. Army testers put the three pilot vehicles through 8,000 miles of the toughest imaginable conditions and found the Willys version to be superior to the others. In November 1940 the Army ordered 1,500 additional models each from Bantam, Willys, and Ford for further testing. The effectiveness of these vehicles convinced the Army to raise the weight specifications to 2,600lb and payload to 800lb.

Another 4,500 units were built by all three suppliers between late 1940 and early 1941 and were put through more exhaustive tests. In all, the Army logged 40 million miles on these 4,500 prototypes and compiled a stack of reports 12ft high. Bantam dropped out of the picture in December of 1941 due to a lack of production capability. Most of the early Bantam jeeps went to Russia. Willys had received the highest ratings in the prototype testing, but Ford was chosen as a second contractor because Willys, too, was a small company and did not have the capacity to build all the light 4x4s the Army would need. Willys sent its blueprints to Ford so that the vehicles would be exactly alike for interchangeability of parts in the field. Ford built about half the 650,000 jeeps produced between 1941 and 1945.

The first 25,000 jeeps had Ford or Willys stamped on the tailgate. A folk legend has it that the back panels were stamped with the manufacturer's name because after the original Bantams were shipped to Russia, the Soviets began boasting that they had invented the jeep. After the Army halted the insignia

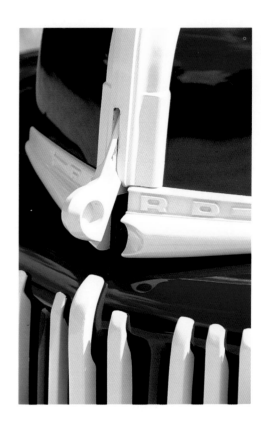

Pulling on the ring in the center of the hood trim operates the hood release. Ford collectors have given the nickname "waterfall" to the vertical grille treatment on 1942-1947 pickups.

practice, Ford continued to stamp bolts for its jeeps with the company's F script on the heads. Ford jeeps can also be recognized by cast brake and clutch pedals. Willys used stampings for these parts. Another difference: Ford used an inverted U-beam front cross-member, while on Willys jeeps the front cross-members are tubular.

Many stories have circulated about the origin of the jeep name. Some say that "jeep" derived from the slurring together of the military designation "GP" for General Purpose vehicle. Others trace the name to a character called Jeep in the popular Popeye cartoon. Whatever the source, the most generally accepted explanation of how the jeep name came to be popularly used is that in March of 1941, Kathryn Hillyer, a reporter for the *Washington Daily News*, took a ride in a jeep that the Army was touring across the country giving demonstrations to the public. After her ride, Ms. Hillyer supposedly asked the Army driver what the machine was

Since Ford also offered a six in its 1942-1947 pickups, on V-8 models the radiator had to be positioned further to the rear in the engine compartment.

called, and he said, "It's a jeep." She used the name in her news story and it stuck. In 1945, seeing a market for the jeep as a civilian vehicle, Willys trademarked the name. The name has since passed to Kaiser, American Motors, and now Chrysler, which aggressively protects its world-famous trademark.

The interior remains stark but functional. Although this truck is fitted with dual windshield wipers, only a single wiper (on the driver's side) was provided as standard equipment. The passenger side wiper was an extra cost option. The 1946 Ford pickup seen in this, and accompanying photos is owned by Sonny Glassbrenner of Largo, Florida.

Chapter 7

1948-1952: Bonus Built Trucks

Along with GM and Chrysler, Ford completely reworked its postwar trucks before restyling its cars. The new truck line, which appeared in January 1948, was the largest in Ford's history and included vehicles from half-ton to 2 1/2- and three-ton extra heavy-duty models. For its expanded truck line Ford adopted a numbering system that started with F-1 representing half-ton models, and proceeded through F-2, F-3, etc.—all the way to F-8 for the heavy-duty three-tonner. This new model identification scheme, which followed a system that International Harvester had been using since 1930, helped buyers and dealers identify the gross vehicle weight ratings of the various models at a glance.

Ford described the new trucks as "Bonus Built." When we think of a bonus we thing of something extra: a "baker's dozen," an extra amount in our paycheck, an extra-generous dividend on an investment. It follows, then, that buyers of Ford's Bonus Built trucks could expect to receive more value for their money than they would find in another manufacturer's product. To see if this was the case, let's look at some of the Bonus

By anyone's standard, Bonus Built Fords are handsome trucks and have been a collector favorite for at least two decades.

In 1948, Ford introduced both an all new truck line and an entirely new numbering system for indicating load rating. Half-ton models were now identified as F-1s. For the light-duty models, the numbering scheme progressed to F-2, indicating a three-quarter-ton load rating, and F-3 for one-ton. The system continued into the medium-duty line, with F-4 indicating ton-and-a-half, and so on.

Built features found on the new F-series Ford trucks.

One of these is what the ad copy called Ford's "Million Dollar Cab." This wasn't just ad hype; Ford had actually spent $1,000,000 to design and tool-up for the new truck cab that offered what Ford salesmen liked to call "Living Room Comfort." Not only did the new cab offer greater inside headroom—a benefit in a day when most truck owners were men and most men wore hats—but it added a full 7in in width, which was a real comfort bonus for three adult men riding together. To make the cab easier to get into and out of, Ford designers moved the front of the door opening ahead 3in to increase the space between the cowl pillar and seat riser. Try to fit a size 12 shoe between the cowl pillar and seat in an earlier truck and you will see how the extra space in that critical area added to the pleasure of owning a new Ford truck.

Brochures for the Bonus Built trucks give considerable emphasis to what the ad writers called "Easy Chair Comfort." Now the familiar bench or "coach" seat could be moved toward or away from the steering wheel to adjust to the driver's height and slid easily on roller bearings. The seat back could also be set for an upright or relaxed posture. Seat cushions constructed of individually pocketed coil springs and padded with

duty three-quarter-ton F-3. The F-1 series consisted of three models: a pickup, panel, and platform/stake body, all on a 114in wheelbase. The pickup box, which measured 6 1/2ft (78in) long, had a metal floor with pressed-in skid strips laid over and offered an enclosed load area of 45 cubic feet.

The panel truck's interior measured 55.4in high by 60in wide, with 95.4in of load space from the rear doors to the back of the driver's seat for a total enclosed load capacity of 160.3 cubic feet. Like the pickup, the platform/stake bed also had a length of 6 1/2 feet but was wider (67in). The factory-supplied stake racks were 29.5in high and were held in place by interlocking plates that allowed their early removal. Due to the fact that the wide bed sat above the tires, lifting height to the platform was 32.6in. All F-1 models carried a GVW (gross vehicle weight) rating of 4,700lb.

All three F-1s offered the 95hp six-cylinder engine as standard equipment; the Flathead V-8, now rated at 100hp, that had nearly become a Ford trademark, could be optioned at extra cost. There were also two transmission choices: a three-speed floor shift was standard, a four-speed optional. The standard tire size was 6.00x16 with 6.50x16 6 ply tires optional.

Ford called its F-2 pickup an express. The other model in this series was the platform/stake. Both were built on a 122in wheelbase. The express box had a length of 8ft while the platform/stake body gave a load length of 7 1/2ft. In this series, too, the six-cylinder engine was standard, V-8 optional. Ford's F-2 models had larger tires (6.50x16), larger brakes and clutch, and a more heavy duty frame, springs, and axles. A four-speed transmission was standard. The F-2 carried a GVW rating of 5,700lb, which translates to a three-quarter-ton load road rating.

The F-3 series also consisted of an express and platform/stake on a 122in wheelbase. These trucks rode on larger (17in) wheels, and had heavier duty axles, brakes, and springs. The F-3 series carried a 6,800lb GVW rating.

There's no quick way to tell a 1949 Ford truck from a 1948 model. If you're concerned whether your Bonus Built Ford is a 1948, 1949, or 1950 (superficially, all three are nearly identical), you'll need to do some detective work

In 1948, Ford introduced its famous F-series. These trucks were literally redesigned from the ground up. The new cab offered what Ford truck salesmen liked to call "Living Room Comfort." The 1948, 1949, and 1950 models of this "Bonus Built" series resemble each other so closely that they're difficult to tell apart.

cotton batting offered the comfort of a favorite living room chair.

The Bonus Built cab also featured "Level Action Cab Suspension," which meant insulated mounts at each front corner and torsion-type rubber bushings at each rear corner, insulating the cab from frame weave. The Level Action anchoring system also dampened out engine and chassis vibration.

For added comfort during warm weather, Ford's Bonus Built trucks offered "three-way air control." In plain terms this amounted to a ventilation system that consisted of vent windows

Previous page
For the first production year (1948), the recessed area around the grille was painted Tucson Tan. For 1949 and 1950 (a 1950 model is seen here) the recessed area is painted aluminum. This, and a few other subtle changes, are all that distinguishes one model year from another.

in the doors, a large cowl ventilator with bug screen that deflected air down on the driver's and passengers' legs and feet, and an optional heater/defroster that circulated fresh air drawn in through a duct running from the heater to an intake vent concealed just above the headlight on the right front fender. In summer, a driver could run just the blower to bathe the truck's occupants with fresh air.

By anyone's standard, Bonus Built Fords are handsome trucks and have been a collector favorite for at least two decades. The recessed grille, combined with gracefully flowing fender contours gives these trucks a streamlined frontal appearance. The rounded frontal lines carried into cab and rear fenders. Wide "shelves" on the tops of the front fenders lend the impression that these trucks are broader than they actually are. Although the one-piece "Safety Vision Windshield" appears small, particularly in comparison with the two-piece windshields used on Dodge and Chevy trucks of the same vintage, it contained greater glass area than windshields on previous model Ford trucks. The back window was also larger.

Ford's light-duty Bonus Built trucks are divided into three series by load rating. Starting with the half-ton class F-1, light-duty models progressed to the three-quarter-ton rated F-2, and heavy-based on minor paint and trim changes. For 1949, wheels were painted body color instead of black; the vent window division bars were now black instead of chrome; the grille recess was painted Aluminum instead of Tucson Tan; and the red pin stripe on the painted grille bars was deleted. If you're trying to determine the year of an early Bonus Built model that has been repainted, you'll find some serial number help at the end of this chapter. Recognizing a 1950 model is easier if the truck has a factory-fitted three-speed transmission. For this year, the gearshift lever to the three-speed gearbox was moved to the steering column.

For 1951, Ford upgraded its trucks with a number of changes and improvements. Probably the most noticeable change is the new grille, which now reached to the edges of both fenders and consisted of a massive bar with pods in the ends that contained the headlights. Three cone-shaped protrusions (referred to as "dagmars") straddled the grille bar between the headlights. The front fenders were also restyled to accommodate the wider grille, and the large "nostril" vents formerly found on the front of the hood were deleted. The Ford name was now stamped into a chrome trim piece on the front of the hood instead of being printed in block letters above the grille. Restyled bumpers that wrapped around more at the ends and were notched in the center for greater strength replaced the former slightly curved channel bumper.

Even more changes can be found inside the cab. The dash layout now placed the instrumentation and speedometer in two separate circular housings. A decorative trim piece housing the grille for the optional radio now extended across the passenger side of the dash, blending with the glove box. Cabs were now available in two trim levels called "5-Star" or "5-Star Extra." The standard 5-Star package continued the features that had been found on Bonus Built Ford trucks since 1948: three-way ventilation, adjustable seat, dual windshield wipers, an ash tray, glove box, and driver's side visor. The deluxe 5-Star Extra package added foam rubber padding on the bench seat, head lining backed by 1 1/2in glass wool padding, additional sound deadener on the doors, cardboard covering on the kick panels and rear cab area,

Panel trucks continued to be popular in the new F-series. The redesigned panel body gave an enclosed load capacity of 160.3 cubic feet, making it a very handy hauler for a variety of cargo.

For 1951, Ford gave its trucks a facelift that replaced the horizontal grille bars with a cavernous frontal opening and a massive single grille bar adorned by three ornamental teeth, or "dagmars," as they were popularly called. Other changes included eliminating the steel floor covering found on previous models' pickup boxes.

two extra chrome bars on the side hood trim, bright metal for the windshield molding, vent window frames and divider bar, Argent (silver) paint on the grille, two-tone seat upholstery, door and body panels, two sun visors, armrests on both doors, a cigar lighter, door locks on each door (and a locking glove compartment), a dome light, and twin horns.

Although today most of the upgrades that appeared with the 5-Star Extra package would be taken for granted, something as ordinary as a passenger-side sun visor or a driver's side door lock, for example, was almost unheard of on a truck in the early fifties. Ford was beginning to give its light trucks car-like convenience features, a move that would ultimately place light trucks ahead of cars on the sales charts.

For 1951, Ford eliminated the steel covering on the floors of its pickup boxes, reverting to hardwood floors protected by steel skid strips. One of the more bragged-about mechanical changes was a vacuum spark advance mechanism called "Power Pilot" that metered fuel and adjusted spark according to load conditions. Although simple in comparison to the electronic spark and fuel metering systems on today's cars, Power Pilot was an early attempt to increase fuel economy and allow lower fuel grades based on the intake manifold's vacuum reading.

Styling changes for 1952 were minimal. The hood's nose vent molding was painted; the Ford nameplate was moved to the cross-bar above the grille as on 1948 through 1950 models; and the series emblem was placed in a round disc forward on the hood side. Engine choice was designated by either a V-8 or 6 insignia in the center of the hood nose molding.

Even though the styling went largely unchanged, Ford announced two big changes to its light duty trucks offerings in 1952. The first came in the form of a totally redesigned six-cylinder engine with overhead valves (a first for Ford). From a 215ci displacement, this new en-

Beginning with 1948, Ford mounted the spare tire under the bed. Although this location puts the tire out of the way, as any pickup owner who has had to change a flat knows, wrestling the spare from its hidden perch is no pleasant task.

gine produced 101hp at 3500rpm. So as not to embarrass buyers of trucks fitted with the old standby Flathead V-8, that engine received a slight power boost from 100hp to 106hp. A significant announcement was an all-new delivery model called the Courier, built on the Ranch Wagon station wagon body. In 1952 the Courier was the best-looking commercial vehicle on the market and came standard equipped with the new ohv six coupled to a three-speed manual; three-speed with overdrive or Ford-O-Matic, and the old Flathead V-8 was optional.

Ford closed out its successful Bonus Built truck series in 1952. Although the high-rounded cab had been in production one year less than the similarly-styled Chevrolet, its one-piece windshield gave it a dated look. To take advantage of the growing light truck market, Ford was preparing a totally re-engineered and restyled truck line for 1953 that would prove to be one of the most popular truck designs of all time.

Bonus Built Pickup Serial Numbers

The serial numbers for 1948 Ford Bonus Built pickups equipped with V-8 engines start at 88RC-101 and end at 88RC-139262. The first 8 is the model year (48), the next 8 and R stand for an eight-cylinder engine, and C stands for half-ton class, while the numbers at the end are the truck's number in the production sequence.

Six-cylinder models use serial numbers 87HC-6911 through 87HC-166969. Again the first 8 is the model year, the 7H indicates the six-cylinder engine, C stands for half-ton, and the digits tell the production sequence.

Ford called trucks in its 1948-1952 styling series "Bonus Built." One of the bonuses a buyer of these trucks received was the "Million Dollar Cab." This wasn't just ad hype; Ford had actually spent $1,000,000 to design and tool-up for the new truck cab that offered what Ford salesmen liked to call "Living Room Comfort." Not only did the new cab offer greater inside headroom—a benefit in a day when most truck owners were men and most men wore hats—but it also added a full 7in in width—a real comfort bonus when three adult men decided to travel together. The 1950 "Bonus Built" pickup example seen in this and accompanying photos is owned by Carl and Frank Childs of Boca Raton, Florida.

The gauge display on Ford's 1948-1950 pickups placed the round speedometer at the left of instrument cluster. In 1951, a new gauge display put the instruments in a second round housing.

Ford began to move its pickups into the deluxe category in 1951 by offering a 5-Star Extra cab (the standard cab was called simply 5-Star). With the deluxe cab buyers got a more comfortable, quieter truck—thanks to added foam padding in the seat and sound deadener in the doors and headliner—as well as amenities such as dual sun visors, armrests, and door locks on each door.

For 1949, V-8 half-ton serial numbers begin at 98RC-73088 (with 9 standing for 1949), while the six-cylinder serial numbers start at 97HC-92251. Looking at the serial number doesn't help identify a 1950 Ford F-1 truck since 1950 models continued the 1949 numbers.

Like sitting on a porch, a pickup seems to invite folks to stop by and talk. "Bet you can haul a lot of these salt blocks in your Ford pickup," the fancy dresser on the left might be saying.

"Yup, I've owned Ford pickups all my life. Never had a bad one!" the fellow in the overalls seems to be saying.

Chapter 8

1953-1956: The Original F-100

Some say it's the most handsome pickup of all times. Unquestionably distinctive, the Ford F-100 series trucks with their tall cab, smartly slanted windshield, and short roof looked ready for action from every angle. Here was a truck that had barely launched its hauling career when it became a favorite of the street rod set. Smart styling, yes, but what really set the F-100 apart was its driver appeal. "Hop in, let's head for the open road," the F-100 seems to beckon. There's no mistaking it—this is a truck that's meant to be driven.

And that's part of the plan. In designing its F-100 series, Ford engineers—for the first time in truck history—made the driver their most important consideration. That foresight paid off, and today the F-100 is among the most highly valued of all light trucks.

The Ford Motor Company celebrated its fiftieth anniversary in 1953. With the revamped postwar car lineup just a year old, the new truck and farm equipment lines held the spotlight. The F-100 carried a family resemblance with the car line; no one would question that the

new trucks were Fords. Yet the Golden Anniversary pickups represented a clean break from their predecessors in every department except the engine choices. Along with a totally restyled cab, Ford's 1953 half-ton pickups sported a longer (6 1/2 ft, or, 78in) and taller (20in) box that can be seen on Ford pickups into the eighties. Keeping pace with the times, the pickup tailgate carried the Ford name in modern block letters. (Formerly the tailgate had carried the Ford name in the company's traditional script.)

Probably the most noticeable feature that sets the F-100 series apart from its predecessors is the expansive window area. In designing Ford's new trucks, stylists increased the windshield area by 55 percent and gave the driver a more panoramic view by making the windshield curved rather than flat. Rear visibility also increased, thanks to a rear window that stretches nearly the width of the cab—a full 4ft. What the ad writers called "armrest" side windows, not only gave F-100 drivers greater lateral visibility, but lowering the window ledges to elbow height also allowed the

Ford F-100 series trucks with their tall cab, smartly slanted windshield, and short roof look ready for action from every angle. These trucks had barely launched their hauling careers when they became a favorite of the hot rod set.

Here's one of the rarest accessories you'll ever see on a 1953 Ford pickup: the factory radio. Truck buyers in the fifties thought of their vehicles strictly as workhorses. Even the ads don't make mention of the radio.

Next page
Keeping pace with the times, the F-100 tailgate displayed the Ford name in modern block letters instead of the traditional script.

driver and passenger to enjoy that relaxing posture of resting an elbow on the window ledge.

"Driver Engineered" is how Ford described the cab of its new truck. The accent here was on comfort—more of it. Inside cab dimensions were stretched to 60.7in (door to door) with a seat to roof height of 36.1in. According to the ad claims, the new wider seat (56.7in) gave "roomy comfort for three men." In making their claim the ad writers weren't using a man's posterior as a yardstick. Unless she was accompanying her husband to town, in 1953 a woman was rarely seen in a truck.

For 1953, the horn button carried the same crest, along with the words "Silver Anniversary," marking Ford's 50th year.

Ford's restyled truck line, introduced in 1953, also received an all-new crest that looked similar to the emblem now used on the car line, but used a distinctive gear and thunderbolt to represent the working side of the Ford family. Trucks equipped with the familiar Flathead eight-cylinder engine continued to be identified by the V8 insignia.

In the eyes of most vintage truck enthusiasts, Ford's 1953-1956 F-100 models have a timeless "classic" appeal. In the mid-fifties there were lots of reasons to own a Ford pickup. The ohv six, introduced in 1952, was a winner, and an all-new ohv V-8 appeared with the 1954 models. It seems that these early F-100 models have been collector trucks from the time they first hit the used car lots. Today there's even an early F-100 club in Japan.

The F-100 cab is more than spacious, and it's better looking. Instead of covering the seat with the moose-nose brown vinyl that had typified pickup interiors for years, Ford now gave its trucks a touch of passenger car class by adding two color-coordinated bands: one across the front cushion and another on the backrest. Of the seat itself, the chief of automotive writers, Tom McCahill, wrote in his test of a 1954 F-100 (*Mechanix Illustrated*, October, 1954): "Inside, the cab has a three-passenger bench seat which is as comfortable as the average sedan's...." Driver Engineered touches also extended to the restyled instrument pod, which grouped the speedometer and full set of gauges for easy visibility in front of the driver.

For 1953, light-duty Ford trucks continued to use the engines that had been offered in 1952, the new 215ci ohv six and the tried-and-true 239ci Flathead V-8. The improved breathing characteris-

Bill Bennett's 1955 Ford F-100 Ohio Bell Telephone Company Service Truck

by Len Kutschman

To a kid who grew up in the fifties, seeing Bill Bennett's 1955 F-100 Bell Telephone Service Truck brought back some fond memories. I was only 7 or 8 at the time, but I remember my best friend Bob's dad driving a similar truck for the Michigan Bell Telephone Company. All the compartments in the utility box were stuffed full of interesting and unique tools and gadgets specific to the trade.

Bill Bennett's truck was built in April 1955, but did not go into service for the Bell System until September 1955. These trucks were built on special order for the American Telephone and Telegraph Company. They were used by the Bell System throughout the country. The color was patented and used exclusively on all Bell System Trucks.

Subsequent to assembly, this particular truck was assigned to the California Bell Telephone Company. Its working life for Bell was spent in and around the San Diego, California, area. When it was retired from its official capacity, it was purchased by a contractor who used it for several years as a field service truck for construction equipment. Subsequently, it was acquired by a farmer who apparently thought he had the perfect retirement setting for the aging vehicle. The truck was nestled out by the barn with both doors thrown open and spent the next seven years of its existence as a dog house. In 1986, however, the truck was rescued from retirement. It was given a second chance at life with a new set of tires, a brake job, and a tune-up, and it journeyed effortlessly from California to its new home in Ohio without a problem.

As the proud new owner, Bill Bennett has begun to restore this truck to original. The interior has been replaced and is an exact duplicate of the original. The exterior, except for the paint, is completely original. The odometer currently indicates slightly less than 50,000 original miles.

Having spent countless hours scrounging through hundreds of garage sales and flea markets, the utility box compartments are once again fully equipped with parts, tools, and equipment of the era. It looks as if Bill's truck could easily be on its way back to the local service center after having been out on call for the last thirty-five years.

Besides the familiar pickup box, Ford light-duty F-100 trucks could be fitted with a variety of utility boxes, including the telephone lineman's equipment box seen on this impeccably restored Bell Telephone truck. This truck's owner has even gone so far as to equip his truck with all the correct vintage telephone technician's tools.

The new F-100 trucks offered a more spacious cab. Inside dimensions gave a 5 1/2ft wide seat. "Roomy comfort for three men" the ads boasted. The 1953 F-100 truck shown in this, and accompanying photos is owned by Rich and Judy Doligale of Chicago, Illinois.

tics of the overhead valve six gave this engine nearly the performance of the V-8 with considerably better fuel mileage. Canadian-built Ford trucks that wore the Mercury nameplate and were designated M-100 instead of F-100 continued to use the old L-head six. Transmission choices now included an automatic transmission, which for 1953 was only available in the half-ton models. Manual transmission offerings included a synchromesh three-speed, three-speed with

overdrive, and four-speed. Both the three- and four-speed manual gearboxes featured synchronizers in the upper gears for smooth, quiet shifting. Actually, two three-speed transmissions were available: the standard gearbox supplied with the F-100 and a heavy-duty unit that was installed in the F-250 and F-350 models. A column shift snapped both three-speed trannies through the gears. In the fifties a column shift was considered a convenience feature for the driver and center passenger. The four-speed gearbox used a floor shifter.

When fitted with either the three-speed or four-speed transmissions, final drive ratios were 3.92 or 4.27 to 1. When overdrive was added, available rear end gearing was 4.09 or 4.27. The automatic

transmission was paired to a 3.92 rear drive ratio. Still lower (higher numerical) ratios were supplied with the F-250 and F-350 models. Since most collectors prefer higher gearing for quieter over the road travel, a combination of 3.92 gears and overdrive would be very desirable, though that match wasn't available from the factory and would mean swapping rear ends or installing an overdrive transmission in a truck that wasn't so equipped originally.

In the half-ton range, as previously mentioned, F-100 replaced the F-1 identification. More substantial reshuffling occurred up the scale as the F-2 and F-3 models were combined in the new F-250. Although the F-250 received a shorter (118in) wheelbase than the former F-2

F-100, the heavier duty F-250 could be ordered either with a cargo box or stake bed, though the F-250's express body was a full eight footer and the stake bed measured 7 1/2ft (90in) long. At the top of the light truck scale, a new F-350 replaced the former F-4. With a wheelbase stretched to 130in, the F-350 was available with either an express body or 9ft (108in) stake bed. Equipped with single rear tires, the F-350s carried a GVW rating of 7,100lb. Duals at the rear gave a 9,500lb GVW. By stretching the chassis and beefing up such components as brakes and springs, plus adding heavier duty tires, Ford arrived at five payload options and three cargo styles (express, stake or platform, and panel) from its three light-duty series. Bare chassis and cowl, or cowl and windshield configurations could be ordered in each series for conversion to a variety of special uses.

Another significant design change for 1953, but one that it takes a sharp eye to spot, is the shorter cab-to-axle distance on Ford's new light trucks. This feature, which Dodge had introduced on the B-series and International adopted on its L series, was accomplished by relocating the front axle 4in to the rear. This reduced the turning radius and improved the weight distribution. Other usually unnoticed changes included relocating the gas tank under the left side of the frame from its earlier mounting inside the cab and widening the front axle tread to 60.55in. Gasoline filler caps on the F-100 and larger series are found on the left rear corner of the cab.

The taller 6 1/2ft (78in) long pickup box used on the F-100 models gave 45 cubic feet of enclosed cargo space. The box itself was assembled by a combination of rivets and bolts that allowed relatively easy replacement of the side panels. Wooden planks continued to be used for the floor, with steel skid strips covering the joints between the boards. As a benefit to drivers, passengers, and bystanders alike, rubber cushions were positioned on each side of the tailgate to prevent rattles. The express box on the larger F-250 and F-350 models was of all bolted construction. Unlike the F-100 pickup box that measured 49in between the side panels, wheel wells intruded into the express box reducing the unobstructed width to slightly over 48in.

Ford continued the standard and deluxe trim and interior package that it

had begun in 1951. On both the pickup and panel delivery, the deluxe package included additional bright work on the outside and color-keyed two-tone upholstery and harmonizing door trim, thicker seat padding, and added sound deadening on the inside. Deluxe pickups had locks on both doors. It had been common practice for years to equip trucks with only a passenger-side door lock. The idea behind this was that truck drivers, as well as passengers, exited on the curbside—not very practical in real life. A lock on both doors was a definite convenience plus. Other deluxe features included dual armrests, a dome light, dual sun visors, bright trim on the dashboard and window ledges, twin horns, a dispatch box lock, and an illuminated cigar lighter. Notice the terms "dispatch box" and "cigar lighter." That's how they're listed in the sales literature. In 1953 when you entered a truck, be it pickup or panel, you entered a man's world. The twin horn feature carries us back, too. With one horn all you get is noise. Two horns are needed for melody, and in a less-hurried time a horn was used to toot at friends more than to honk a path through traffic.

The deluxe panel truck added masonite lining on the sides of the cargo area, full-length roof paneling, sound deadener in the floor and above the headliner, and a foam padded driver's seat. Extras included a rear bumper (standard in the panel delivery), tinted glass, heater and defroster, heavy duty springs, and six-ply 6.00x16 or oversize tires.

At a glance Ford light trucks from 1953-1955 all look alike. The end-of-series 1956 F-100 with its "panoramic" wraparound windshield is easy to spot. Learning the different grille treatments is the easiest way to tell the earlier years apart. For 1954, two angular supports (somewhat reminiscent of the 1951-1952 dagmars) attach the horizontal grille bar, inboard of the headlights. In 1955, the grille consisted two parallel bars, the upper bar having a deep V-shaped notch in the center .

For 1954 the big news was the new "Y" block overhead valve (ohv) V-8 engine. A downsized version of the ohv V-8 that had been used in Lincoln cars and Ford heavy-duty trucks since 1952, this engine displaced 239ci and developed 130hp. As developments over the next

few years would prove, this engine had been designed with plenty of growth and performance potential. In its introductory year the new engine had a mild 7.2:1 compression ratio and was fitted with a two-barrel carburetor.

Though overshadowed by the new V-8, the six-cylinder engine also saw redesign for 1954. Opening the bore to 3.62in boosted displacement to 223ci. Stroke stayed the same at 3.60in, resulting in a low-wear, "oversquare" design. Upping the compression ratio to 7.2:1 gave a horsepower jump to 115hp at 3900rpm. In six-cylinder form, the F-100 was economical to operate and could be driven off a dealer's lot for under $1,600—a lot of truck even for 1954 dollars. The V-8 carried a premium of almost $100.

Other changes for 1954 were largely convenience upgrades. Seat upholstery was now woven vinyl for longer wear. The Ford-O-Matic transmission could now be optioned in the F-250 and single wheel F-350 as well as in the F-100 and Courier sedan delivery. Other options included four-leaf auxiliary rear springs and power brakes on the F-100 as well as a side-mounted spare for the pickup and express bed models. Engines were now painted yellow (through 1953 engines had been painted green).

While Chevrolet chose 1955 as the year to introduce its completely restyled "Task Force" trucks, Ford continued to refine its existing models. Tubeless tires were adopted by the automotive industry in 1955 and replaced tube-type tires on the F-100 that year. Standard tire size remained 6.00x16. Other changes included a slight horsepower boost to 132bhp on the Y-block V-8 and to 118bhp on the I-6. Ford engines of this period were cast with deep skirt extensions that gave substantial main bearing and crankshaft rigidity. When you look at a fifties vintage Ford ohv V-8 block, you'll notice that the casting has a distinct "Y" appearance. That's the reason for the Y-block reference. The six-cylinder block also extends below the centerline of the crankshaft; thus the I-block reference.

Colors for 1955 fell in the "cool" range with three new blues and a soft green. The Custom cab could now be ordered in a two-tone combination of any body color plus a white roof and upper back panel. The grille bars were now painted off-white, along with the wheels,

For 1956, Ford gave its trucks a wraparound windshield. This styling change has made the 1956 models the most popular of the original F-100 series. Even more significant than styling was Ford's decision to update its 1956 models to a 12-volt electrical system. Earlier models with the 6-volt electricals can be upgraded to 12 volts quite easily using a 1956 generator and other electrical parts.

which were now white rather than body color.

The Deluxe models were now called "Custom" and had several new dress-up features including "Custom" nameplates on the doors, a bright metal drip rail, chrome upper grille bar, and stainless steel vent window frames. Optional two-stage rear springs boosted the F-100's GVW to 5,000lb. As a convenience feature, a key switch now activated the starter instead of a push button. As is sometimes the case, not all "improvements" were for the better. "Idiot" lights

now replaced oil pressure gauge and ammeter.

On the F-250 series, power brakes were now an option and a Spicer Model 60 rear axle replaced the Timken axle traditionally used in heavier duty Ford trucks. Load rating on the F-350 increased by 600lb to 7,700lb GVW (on the single wheel models). These trucks also offered the power brake option. A record number of 373,897 (all models) Ford trucks were produced in calendar year 1955, beating the company's previous production record set in 1929.

Major restyling for Ford's truck line would wait for 1957, so in an attempt to keep its trucks from wearing what, at the time, seemed the hopelessly outdated curved but not "wrapped around" windshield, Ford stylists played "me too" and applied a hasty facelift that bent the windshield pillars back to horizontal. The vent windows were squared off and the roof was extended somewhat to meet the less-slanted windshield. The effect

did little to enhance the "clean" F-100 design.

At the rear of the cab Ford also offered a wraparound window. The big rear window option helped integrate the new cab's styling and today this is a highly desirable feature; some owners have actually converted their trucks from the standard to the panoramic rear window. Other attempts to update the four year old design included recessing the headlights into the grille. "Frenched" or hooded headlights had originated as a customizing fad, but by 1956 could be found on nearly all domestic cars and most light trucks. A smart-looking hooded instrument cluster that closely resembled the Ford car layout replaced the former gauge pod that Tom McCahill had described in his 1954 Ford F-100 road test as "untiringly nice and plain." The accessory list now described a chrome-plated grille as a dress-up item.

Ford made two significant safety improvements to its cars and light trucks for 1956 and made safety the focus of its ad campaign. Oddly, the safety features seemed to have no effect on sales. The safety items consisted of a deeply dished steering wheel that helped protect the driver from chest injuries in a head-on crash and interlocking door latches that were less likely to pop open on impact. Because of the public's lackluster response, industry-wide safety improvements would wait for the consumer advocate movement of the sixties.

By 1956 nearly all US-made vehicles had converted to 12 volt electrical systems and the new Ford trucks were no exception. The change from 6 to 12 volts gave snappier starting, particularly with the V-8 engines that now had a compression ratio of 7.8:1, and increased the capacity for electrical accessories. Besides the revamped electrical system, other changes included a longer 8ft pickup bed for the F-100 line and 15in wheels replacing the former 16in rims. Standard tire size was now 6.70x15. Since the series was reaching the end of its run, rather than design a new frame to accommodate the longer box, the lighter trucks were simply fitted with frames from the F-250 models. For 1956, the gas tank, which had been relocated outside the cab in 1953, was moved back inside.

Chevrolet's introduction of its hot V-8 in 1955 locked the number one and number two car and light truck makers in a performance duel that continues to this day. Improved manifolding and higher compression boosted the six to 133bhp at 4000rpm, but real fuel for the horsepower race came in the form of the 272ci V-8, rated at 167hp. The higher output engines gave Ford trucks the needed pulling power for the increased cargo capacity of the 8ft box now available on the F-100 pickup, and GVW ratings raised to 7,400lb and 8,000lb on the F-250 and F-350 single rear wheel models.

The Panel Delivery continued as an F-100 offering, and today a 1956 panel truck is the most sought-after model of the series, perhaps because of its throwback styling that blended the wraparound windshield with running boards and trendy "fat" fenders. Both the Panel and pickup continued to be available in both standard and custom trim packages. For 1956, Custom features included a chrome grille, bright metal windshield molding, and dash and inner door trim. Plated vent window frames were no longer offered. Custom upholstery used an attractive black and white chain-stripe weave with red or copper-toned facing.

Besides its light trucks, Ford also offered its station wagon-based Courier sedan delivery. For 1953, the car line underwent a minor face lift that is noticeable mainly in a slightly reworked grille that had three vertical stripes on each side of what was now a solid spinner. Along with the trucks, the Courier dis-played the 50th Anniversary medallion on the horn button. At a base cost of $1,570, the 1953 Courier was priced the lowest of all Ford's automotive offerings and set a production record of 10,575 units.

Both the Ford truck line and the Courier delivery received all new styling for 1957. On trucks, the new look can be described simply as squared-off and slab sided.

F-100 Production Figures

1953
Pickup	116,437
Std. Panel	9,951
Del. Panel	2,000
Courier	10,575

1954
Pickup	101,202
Std. Panel	8,078
Del. Panel	1,015
Courier	6,404

1955
Pickup	124,842
Std. Panel	11,198
Del. Panel	1,076
Courier	7,754

1956
Pickup	137,581
Std. Panel	14,023
Del. Panel	1,190
Courier	8,757

Chapter 9

1957-1960: Refrigerator Styling

When Ford stylists created the new truck line that would appear in 1957, two factors guided their design. First, the trucks were to look totally modern. Gone would be the outdated separate fenders, high-crowned hood, and running boards. The new trucks would adopt an integrated design whereby the cab and box would reflect a unit—like a car, instead of the traditional two-piece truck design. By adopting the new wide Styleside box as standard equipment, Ford had an offering that none of the other truck lines could match. The second guideline was to establish a clear family connection between the car and truck lines.

It's easy to see how the stylists accomplished their first goal. Overall height of the new pickups dropped 3 1/2in. Fenders, both front and rear, completely disappeared on the wide-box Styleside models. The hood now covered the tops of the front fenders and its flat surface made for excellent forward visibility. An inboard step that was concealed by the doors replaced the running boards. (This concealed step design wasn't new; Studebaker had introduced it in

1949 and Chevrolet had followed in 1955.) Ford's new truck line was so radically restyled that the only link to the previous models was the grille and headlight bar, which retained sufficient similarity to the 1956 nosepiece to keep the new trucks in the Ford family. Unquestionably, Ford's 1957 trucks were modern and easy to spot on the road, but how, you ask, did they make a styling link with the new Ford car line?

For buyers wanting added interior styling and comfort, Ford offered the Custom Cab, which featured brighter upholstery colors, thicker seat padding, dual sun visors, locks on both doors, and added soundproofing.

The styling bridge between Ford's 1957 cars and trucks is subtle, but it's there. For starters, compare the fender flares over the wheel cutouts. OK, so the fender flares on the cars are concave indents rather than the squarish relief moldings on the trucks, but both serve to dramatize the wheel cutouts. Next, note the windshield resemblance. It's true that the truck's windshield pillars don't sweep as far back as the car's, but the windshield look is unmistakably Ford in both cases.

Although Ford's 1957 truck lineup, from the appealing new Ranch-ero to the pace-setting Styleside pickups and on up through the medium and heavy-duty models, was distinctively modern, to many present-day collectors, the boxy lines looked better on the big trucks than the pickups. Perhaps the reason for the squared-off lines on Ford's 1957-1960 pickups is that the "massive look" had become the dominant styling theme. Bigger is better—so said the wisdom of the time. The exaggerated "dagmar" cones protruding from Cadillac bumpers of the era are a case in point. Given the prevailing styling sense, the wide flat hood and slab sides on Ford's new trucks weren't at all out of place in 1957. And the new Styleside box helped play out the massive, boxy styling theme from grille to tailgate. That's why you could call it "refrigerator" styling.

The chrome grille and bumpers, wide rear window, whitewall tires, full wheel covers, and side-mounted spare seen on this truck were all extra-cost options.

Chevrolet had pioneered the smooth-sided pickup box with Cameo Carrier, introduced in 1955. Actually, though, the smooth sides on the Cameo box were an illusion created by full-length fiberglass fenders grafted onto an old-style narrow box. For 1957, Ford one-upped Chevy on the home court by giving its trucks a true wide box. Unlike Chevrolet, Ford placed the wheel housings inside the cargo area and opened the cargo space to nearly the full width of the box. Sales brochures boasted that the wide box added up to 45 percent more load space. The Styleside box was standard—at no extra cost. Ford still offered the traditional narrow-box pickup, but few examples were seen when the trucks were new, and fewer still are found today.

When designers develop a new styling theme, they still face the challenge of retaining just enough of the former product's look so that there's no mistaking whose vehicle this is. The grille and headlight bar provided that link for the new Ford trucks; just about every other feature (except the emblems) was changed. Eliminating the channel-bar bumpers of the 1953-1956 series, the new Fords carried simple yet stylish bumpers that wrapped around the corners of the front fenders. Circular parking lights mounted under the headlights marked the outer boundary of the lower grille opening. The Ford insignia used since the Golden Anniversary 1953 models (a Ford crest inset with a gear shish kebabbed by a lightning bolt) decorated the hood lip. On top, the hood wore a series of stamped grooves that served a functional (if not a decorative) purpose by strengthening the large, otherwise flat, hood expanse. So large is the hood's flat expanse that it could have been used as a forward cargo deck if such a use wouldn't have obstructed the driver's view of the road. Along the sides of the truck, a styling crease that ran from the top of the headlight pod to just above the round taillights made a dividing point for the new two-tone color schemes. No longer was the contrasting white applied to the roof and cab pillars only. Now

Although the wide, Styleside box was standard at no extra-cost. Buyers could still choose the traditional, fendered box seen on this 1960 Custom Cab F-100 pickup owned by Ralph Westcott of Largo Florida.

By the sixties, truck buyers were starting to become style conscious. Ford addressed this trend by supplying full disk wheel covers and whitewall tires as extra cost options.

when a buyer specified a two-tone color scheme, the body color extended up to the beltline crease and also covered the roof cap. A contrasting white highlighted the upper body and hood, cab pillars, and a sculpted panel that arched above the doors and crossed the roof behind the windshield header.

Ford's new "Driverized" pickup cabs featured Hi-Dri ventilation (meaning that the air vents were mounted on top of the cowl), a full 59in of shoulder room, a seat width of 63 1/8in, a 61.5in wide panoramic windshield, and optional wide rear window. Combining the "full-wrap" windshield and rear window with the truck's squared-off styling made it easy for the driver to keep tabs on all four corners of the vehicle in parking and maneuvering through tight spaces. Other cab improvements included

checks to hold the doors in a partially opened position, a redesigned instrument panel that arranged the gauges and idiot lights simply, but attractively, around a central speedometer, and suspended brake, clutch, and accelerator pedals. Pedals whose mounting bracket attached to the firewall had appeared on cars in 1955 with claims that the "swing" action made the pedals easier to work. On trucks, the sales brochures pointed to another advantage: suspended pedals didn't require drafty holes in the cab floor. Ford advertised its 1957 trucks as having the strongest, sturdiest light-duty cabs ever with the Ford name. Floor pans stamped from 18-gauge steel helped substantiate that claim.

In 1957, Ford continued to lead the industry in safety consciousness. Besides the deep dished "safety" steering wheels introduced in 1956, double-grip door locks and rearview mirrors were installed on all Ford trucks. A padded dash could also be specified, as well as seatbelts. The latter were dealer-installed. Seat coverings were now a two-toned tan and brown woven plastic that was more comfortable in hot weather, easier to clean, and longer wearing. Custom cab trucks featured brighter colored upholstery consisting of red and white or green and white weave with seat facings and bolster in a matching vinyl. Seats in Custom cab trucks contained a full 5in of foam rubber in the cushion and 2in of foam in the backrest. Other Custom cab extras included dual sun visors, an illuminated cigar lighter, matched key locks on both doors, and perforated headlining backed by a 1/2in of glass wool sound deadener.

Beyond its styling appeal, the new wide box offered several practical advantages. For easier loading and unloading, the tailgate opened level with the floor and the tailgate opening measured 50.2in. Boxed rear corner posts assured structural durability as did the metal floor. On the F-100 model both 6 1/2ft (78in) and 8ft (96in) boxes were available. Due to the boxy styling that emphasized the truck's width and the long flat hood, the short 6 1/2ft box looked somewhat stubby and out-of-proportion. Ford fitted only the F-250 with the 8ft box; the F-350 came with a 9ft (108in) box.

The old-style narrow box, now called the "Flareside," became a special-order item. Trucks fitted with the Flareside box also had a short running board between the cab and the rear fender. The Flareside box was available in the same lengths as the Styleside version. Side height of the longer 8ft and 9ft boxes measured 22in compared with 20in on the 6 1/2ft short box.

Engines for Ford's 1957 light trucks consisted of the 223ci I-block six and the 272ci Y-block V-8. Duly noted in company advertising was the fact that Ford offered the only modern short-stroke six in its field. Chevrolet's long-stroke six had been introduced in 1932, and Dodge was still using its dated L-head six. The Ford six now had a rating of 139hp while the V-8 now produced 172hp. Color schemes differed for the two engines. Engine castings on the six were painted red with blue valve covers and accessories. The Y-block V-8 was painted yellow, with black valve covers and accessories. Ford-O-Matic transmission was optional, as were power brakes.

In keeping with the increased emphasis on styling and comfort, light-truck buyers were treated to accessory lists that seemed to grow longer each year. For 1957, Ford-authorized extra-cost items included: a radio, windshield washers, outside rearview mirror, seat covers, spot light, directional signals, grille guard, a four-speed synchromesh transmission (F-100 and F-250), 11in clutch, heavy-duty floor mats, front tow hooks, bright metal hub caps, a locking gas cap, heavy-duty radiator, chrome bumpers front and rear, a right side taillight (on the narrow Flareside box), side-mounted tire and tire lock, and—!—an

My Pickup Truck Experiences
by Ted Pollari

Before 1957, pickup trucks were just that. A third passenger was more comfortable riding in the cargo box. With the 1957 models came wider, softer seats, wraparound windshields, two-tone paint, and so on. They looked good enough to take on a Sunday drive with all the members of a family sitting on the seat. In 1957 I needed a second car so I chose a new Ford F-100 with all the extras except the wide wraparound rear window. I ordered it with overdrive, red and white paint, tinted glass, chrome mirrors and bumpers, and the Custom Cab. It cost $1,978.80. The overdrive made the truck economical and a pleasure to drive. I thought I would own it forever.

In 1962 my brother helped me move, and for compensation he talked me into selling my pickup to him. It so happened that there was a 1962 F-100 in the Hiawatha, Kansas, Ford dealer's showroom. It had all the same extras as my '57 except overdrive. This new truck cost $1,911.63 (after some dickering), so the pain of losing the '57 was eased a little.

After moving off our farm in 1967, we sold the pickup and attempted to get along with one car. Within a year I was driving a 1965 IH (International) pickup, but it used so much gas I traded it for a VW. In 1985, we went to my forty-fifth high school class reunion and visited my brother near Vancouver, Wyoming. He still had *my* 1957 F-100 and suggested that I buy it back. Since his son would not release the title and they disagreed about the ownership, I returned home and bought a 1965 Ford F-100 to stop a family argument. And so I became a pickup owner again.

One day in June 1987 my wife came home and told me that she had seen a "For Sale" sign on a pickup that I should look at (she is the kind of wife all pickup lovers should have). It was a 1963 F-100 six cylinder with separate cargo box—the standard '63 F-100 had the unitized cab and box. The engine ran after a jump start but had a bad miss. The hood had to be propped open with a stick and there was a nightmare of 14 guage building wire in parallel with the wiring harness. Even the steering column had many wraps of wire around it. The cargo box floor was badly rusted, but that pickup sat with one flat tire like a lost puppy looking for someone to pet him and take him home. So for $250 I became the new owner.

The original wiring harness just needed cleaning up, some connections, and a good ground circuit between body parts. The engine had one burned valve and after a valve job it purrs like a kitten. I enrolled in welding classes at the local technical college and am making a sheet metal brake of my own design to form parts to repair the cargo box.

Decoration on late-fifties cars and trucks often had a futuristic touch, as seen in the "stars" placed on either side of the instrument cluster on this 1960 Ford pickup.

electric shaver. Standard tire size for the F-100 was 6.70x15 with a four-ply rating; heavier duty six-ply tires were available by special order.

In its F-100 line, Ford also offered stake and platform models plus the familiar panel truck, which was available both in a standard and Custom model. The panel truck carried the boxy lines better than the pickups. The squared-off styling maximized the load space, which now totaled 158 cubic feet. With the floor space beside the drivers seat added in, load length totaled 130.6in. The rear doors opened a full 180 degrees to expose a cavernous 61.5x45.9in cargo opening. The panel truck featured a plywood floor with skid strips for easy loading. Custom panel features included sound deadener on the headliner over the driver's compartment, masonite lining in the cargo area, as well as the dec-

orative trim also found on the Custom pickups. Eight two-tone paint combinations were included in the color options. The two-tone paint scheme consisted of any standard color for the lower body with Colonial white applied to the upper body. What made the two-tone trucks particularly attractive was a continuation of the body color onto the upper door frame and roof revel over the doors and windshield, in effect highlighting the cab portion of the panel body. Mechanical specifications for the F-100 series trucks also applied to the panel.

1958 Trucks

For 1958, Ford dispensed with the grille bar and single headlights that had been a link to the earlier models and adopted a modern grid-style grille with quad headlights. Apart from a different model emblem on the side of the hood over the front wheel cutouts, in external appearance the 1958 pickup is identical to the 1957 model. Mechanical features are also largely unchanged. By midyear, a larger 292ci V-8 rated at 186hp was offered in place of the 272ci version.

In the absence of significant styling or mechanical changes, sales literature boasted that a Ford truck buyer could choose from 306 models. This selection included the larger trucks plus the car-based Courier and Ranchero and included every body combination (pickups, panel, stake, platform, cab chassis, windshield chassis, cowl chassis), wheelbase, cargo length, and engine option. Altogether sixty-six variations existed in the light truck category alone.

1959 Trucks

Ford's 1959 light trucks are relatively easy to recognize. A simple row of horizontal bars, looking like a custom accessory from a J.C. Whitney catalog, replaced the former egg crate grille. The parking lights were now rectangular instead of round, and the hood was also mildly restyled with a dished nose that now carried the Ford lettering in place of the crest. The model designation was moved about a foot back on the hood and consisted of the Ford crest with a gear shish kebabbed by a thunderbolt. In place of the ridge pattern seen on 1957 and 1958 models, the restyled hood used a raised center section that ran all the way back from the nose to strengthen the wide expanse of metal.

For the first time, the Ford truck lineup listed four-wheel-drive pickups. Four-wheel-drive had long been available to Ford pickup owners in the form of

The chief trademark of Ford's 1957-1960 trucks is their boxy styling. One of the most significant advances of this series was the adoption of a full-width pickup box (called the Styleside) as standard equipment. Buyers could still specify the old-style fendered box, but most preferred the roomier, slab-sided box. A notable feature of the truck shown here is four-wheel-drive—an option that Ford pioneered through its linkup with Marmon-Herrington.

Marmon-Herrington conversions, but Ford now made all-wheel-drive a production option.

1960 Trucks

This would be the last year for Ford's square styling trucks, and only minor detail changes can be seen. The badge emblem returned to the front of the hood, joined by two vent slots. A bar connected the quad headlight pods, and the grille now covered the opening just above the bumper. Parking lights were integrated into the far corners of the grille. Mechanical changes were also minor, the most notable being a new heater that was reportedly 10 percent more effective than the unit it replaced, and multiple plug wiring connectors that simplified electrical assembly and re-

FORD F-100 PICKUP FACTS

A completely new concept in pickup design with a functional purpose.
110"-118" W.B.

FACTS

- Max. GVW 5000 lbs. (½ Ton Pickup).
- Recommended body and payload weight 2028 lbs.
- New exclusive-Styleside body.
- Pickup body capacities up to 70.5 cu. ft.
- 3½" lower than 1956 models.
- 2" wider than 1956 models.
- Choice of automatic or standard transmissions.
- Choice of four half-ton pickups:
  - F-100—6½' Styleside with steel floor.
  - F-100—6½' Flareside with wood floor.
  - F-100—8' Styleside with steel floor.
  - F-100—8' Flareside with wood floor.

FEATURES

- New outstanding Ride

- Longer and wider springs.
- Fewer leaves for less inter-leaf friction.
- New concept in pickup with Styleside bodies with 25% greater bulk space than 1956 bodies. 6½' Body—56.05 cu. ft. 8' body—70.55 cu. ft.
- New suspended pedals for ease of operation, eliminating holes in the floor keeping out dust, road fumes, cold air.
- New hydraulic actuated clutch. The only truck in its class with this exclusive feature. Ease of operation, eliminating clutch chatter, easier servicing.
- New king pins and a larger spindle diameter for *greater durability* and steering ease.
- Wrap-around windshield 2" wider than 1956 models.
- Widest standard rear window in the industry.

For 1957 and Years Ahead—FORD TRUCKS Cost Less—
Less to own . . . Less to run . . . Last Longer, Too!

pair. A heavy-duty Cruise-O-Matic was available in the F-250, F-350 series. Structurally, the frame cross-members were widened. The V-8 engine was now painted blue, with white valve covers and black accessories.

As had been the case in 1956, by 1960 Ford's truck styling was outdated. For 1960, Chevrolet had given its trucks a bold, futuristic look to match the General Motors car lines. Ford's car lines were also restyled for 1960, but the new look was nondescript in that it dropped

In sales literature such as this facts card, Ford said of its new trucks: "They're Boldly Modern for 1957!" And there was plenty of data provided to back up that claim.

all the familiar Ford hallmarks—particularly the "bullet" taillights. As a result, in 1960, no link remained between Ford's car and truck lines. The heavy, boxy styling that hadn't been entirely successful now looked worn. The time had come for a change.

Chapter 10

1961-1966: Becoming Modern

Major truck styling and engineering developments have occurred, on the average, once a decade. As an example, between 1947 and 1949, all major manufacturers thoroughly restyled and introduced new engineering features on their trucks lines. Although Ford redesigned its truck line twice during the next decade and Chevrolet introduced a new truck line in 1955 plus a face-lift in 1958, industrywide styling and major engineering changes didn't occur again until the end of the fifties. International kicked off this round of changes by bringing out the all-new A-line in mid-1957 to celebrate its fiftieth anniversary as a truck builder. Dodge announced its high-style Sweptside the same year, and Ford upped the ante with the all-new Ranchero. In 1959 Chevrolet introduced the El Camino, its Ranchero challenger, and in 1960 Dodge, Chevy, and Stude-

Although Ford's 1965 pickups are best identified by an open-lattice grille and parking lights set just under the front hood opening, the big changes were hidden. Besides the all-new independent front suspension, buyers could choose between three new engines: the standard 240ci six rated at 150hp; the optional 300ci "Big Six," producing 170hp; and the 352ci V-8, rated at 208hp. The V-8-powered example shown here is owned by Mike and Bern Bucher of Pacific, Missouri.

In 1965, Ford introduced a unique type of independent front suspension that retained the basic engineering of an old-fashioned beam axle, but added coil springs and mounted one end of the "I beam" axles on a pivot. The result was a rugged, relatively inexpensive suspension system that allowed either front wheel to roll over bumps without transferring road shock to the other.

baker all announced new truck lines—and still there was more to come.

Dramatic as the first round of new postwar trucks had been, the models unveiled at the end of the fifties represented even bigger changes. Chevy and GMC's light- and heavy-duty trucks acquired independent front suspension, as did International's light-duty models. Dodge finally abandoned its twelve-year-old cab, once again placing its trucks in a competitive stance. Studebaker crafted a new truck cab from the popular Lark car, giving this troubled company's truck line a much needed boost. Ford had revamped its truck line in 1957, and by 1960 the boxy "refrigerator" styling was looking dated, especially on the light trucks. To be competitive in the fast-paced sixties, Ford also needed a restyle—and that's what its trucks got in 1961. So sweeping were the changes to Ford's light trucks that *Motor Trend* magazine called 1961 the "...most important year ever in small truck development."

A year earlier, Ford and GM had awakened from their slumber to meet the import challenge (coming primarily from Volkswagen) with the new compact Falcon and Corvair cars. Now the domestic compacts were extended to include trucks. Ford's small truck entry, the Econoline, adopted cab-forward styling and the Falcon engine/drive-

Previous page
On early models in Ford's 1961-1966 styling series, the box and cab were one unit. This design saved some stamping costs (the rear of the cab served as the front of the box) and provided a slightly longer than normal cargo space, but it also had offsetting disadvantages—particularly when these trucks began to rust. In 1964, the separate box shown here replaced the integral cab/box construction.

In the sixties, large-displacement engines with plenty of horsepower had as much appeal to light truck buyers as they did to new car shoppers.

train, a combination that proved to be a popular seller. The Ranchero, too, became a compact as Ford moved its car/pickup into the Falcon line. Not to be overlooked, the full-sized trucks from Dearborn were also all new.

Once again, Ford managed to preserve a "family resemblance" between its new F-series full-sized light trucks and their boxy predecessors. Features that helped preserve the Ford look were the two-tone paint scheme with the lower body color also applied to the roof and back of the cab, the wide grille, and accent arches over the fender wells. Yet the differences far outweighed the similarities. The severely vertical windshield post was canted forward, glass area was expanded by increasing the window height (the rear glass alone was 28 percent larger), and the angular lines were softened. The new truck styling now bore a closer family resemblance to Ford's car line.

For all their success, the new F-series Fords had one design quirk that didn't make it. Some call it a flaw; to others it's a collector's prize. That design quirk was the integral cab/box Styleside pickup. Since the earliest light trucks were created by bolting a cargo box on back of a roadster tub, it was assumed that pickups had to be of the two box design: a box up front for the driver and passengers to ride in, and a box on the back for the cargo. From 1961 to 1963, Ford's Styleside trucks consisted of just one box with the pickup bed and fenders actually an extension of the cab.

In concept, the integral cab/box pickup was a great design. By eliminating the space between the cab and bed (making the rear of the cab the head of the bed), a longer cargo area could be achieved from the same wheelbase and overall length. Further, the integral cab/box pickup's styling looked great. Because there weren't two boxes to twist and turn independently as the truck

Besides softening its truck styling by making the contours more rounded and flowing, for 1961 Ford experimented with an integral cab/box pickup body. As can be seen in this example, the integral body trucks have continuously flowing side panels from the doors to the rear of the truck. The idea behind making the cab and box all one unit was to get more cargo space by making the rear of the cab the front of the pickup box. However, trucks with this design presented problems, particularly when the bodies began to rust. The truck seen here is owned by Gary Henson.

By 1964, Ford eliminated the integral cab/box approach to its Styleside trucks, returning to the traditional separate box. Another turning point in light truck design also occurred in 1964, with that year marking the end of the rigid front axle.

rolled over bumps, the one-piece trucks also gave a smoother, quieter ride.

In time, problems with this design emerged. Owners in the rust belt found that once the bodies on their integral cab/box Ford pickups started to corrode, the usual remedy—discard the box and replace it with a homebuilt platform—wouldn't work. Rust brought many 1961-63 Ford Styleside pickups to an early end. There were also reports that when loaded, the doors would bind and couldn't be opened. Many owners dispute this, but whether rumor or fact, talk of this sort scared buyers away.

Of course the integral cab/box Styleside model wasn't Ford's only full-sized pickup offering. The Flareside (narrow box) pickups was also made in all three light truck series: F-100 (5,000 GVW), F-250 (7,400 GVW), and F-350 (9,800 GVW). Both the Styleside and Flareside were available with three length boxes: 6 1/2, 8, and 9 feet; however, the 9-foot box was available only in the F-350 series. In the F-100 and F-250 series, a four-wheel-drive Flareside version was also available.

Once again Ford boasted that its trucks were "Driverized" for comfort. What this meant for the 1961-66 models was larger window glass and tandem-action windshield wipers that made parallel sweeps to clear the center of the windshield as well as the area just in front of the driver and passenger. Two trim levels, called "standard" and "deluxe," were also continued. Both the standard and deluxe cabs used a functional "moose-nose brown" seat covering, but on the deluxe models the seats had a fancier twill pattern with imitation-leather facings. Other amenities on the deluxe model included a left-side arm rest, cigar lighter, right side sun visor,

work or play: starring

STYLESIDE! Two-front-axle ride!

Ford's pickup ad boasting two front axles sought to focus prospective buyers' attention on one of the biggest breakthroughs in light truck development—the adoption of independent front suspension (IFS) and a consequent car-like ride.

1961 Ford F-Series Specifications

	F-100	F-200	F-300
GVW	5,000lb	7,400lb	9,800lb
Axle ratio			
6 cyl	3.22, 3.72,	4.88, 5.14, 5.83	3.89, 4.11
8 cyl	3.22, 3.70, 3.89	4.56	4.86, 5.14
Brake lining area	169.2sq in	209.4sq in	238sq in
Engine			
Standard	135hp 223 six	same	same
Optional	160hp 292 V-8	same	same
Transmission	3-speed	3-speed	3-speed
Optional	3-speed OD	3-speed	HD 3-speed
	MD 3-speed	4-speed	HD 3-speed
	4-speed	HD Cruise-O-Matic	Ford-O-Matic
Tire size	6.70 x 15	6.50 x 16	8.17.5 6 PR

Colors: Montecarlo Red, Goldenrod Yellow, Raven Black, Mint Green, Holly Green, Caribbean Turquoise, Academy Blue, Starlight Blue, and Corinthian White. Two-tone available by combining any color with Corinthian White (F-100 and F-250 Styleside pickups only).

driver side door lock, and Custom emblem on the outside of the door. The truck buying public was changing and reflecting that change, Ford's new deluxe cab models also offered a coat hook and insulation on the cowl wall to cut down engine noise.

Engine options for the light-duty F-series (F-100, F-250, and F-350) trucks included the 135hp, 223ci six and the 160hp, 292ci V-8. Both engines were of the short stroke design. Buyers could opt for the standard three-speed transmission or select from a number of transmission options that included overdrive (F-100), medium-duty three-speed (F-100, 250), heavy-duty three-speed (F-350), four-speed (all models), Ford-O-Matic (F-100), or heavy-duty Cruise-O-Matic (F-250, 350). The F-100 wore 6.70x15 tires, while the F-250 was fitted with 6.50x16s.

Included among the new features was an "instant action" tailgate latch on the Styleside pickups. This latch was operated from the left and right sides of the tailgate. Noisy tailgate chains had been replaced by hinged support arms. On the Flareside pickups, short running boards were installed between the cab and rear fenders to make loading and unloading forward cargo easier. Flareside pickups continued to use chains to support and latch the tailgate.

Four-wheel-drive was available in both the F-100 and 250 series, though only with the Flareside box. Like Chevrolet 4x4 trucks of the same era, Ford mounted the transfer case at about the midpoint of the chassis, resulting in a relatively high body. The 4x4 models were built only on a special 120-inch wheelbase.

1962 Trucks

Few differences distinguish Ford's 1961 and 1962 full-sized pickups, the most noticeable being relocation of the Ford name, which is moved from the center of the grille on the 1961 trucks to above the grille on the 1962 models. Base cost of the 1962 pickups dropped a dollar to $1,939. As in 1961, the F-100 models were available on both a short 114-inch and longer 122-inch wheelbase. The F-250 came only in the 122-inch length, while the F-350 used a longer 132-inch wheelbase. Two box lengths (6 1/2 and 8ft) were offered with the F-100 and 250, while the F-350 used a 9ft box. As in 1961, besides the Styleside or Flareside pickups, platform/stake, chassis cab, chassis-cowl, and chassis-windshield configurations were available.

1963 Trucks

Although Ford retained the integral cab/box styleside design through 1963, for this year only, both integral and separate wide boxes were offered. Clearly Ford had not planned to drop the integral box after just two years and had not prepared tooling for a separate wide box, so the 1957-60 Styleside box was used. Since the earlier box had more angular wheel cutout flares, the mismatch calls attention to itself. Even so, the separate Styleside box was an extra cost option. Both the separate and integral Styleside boxes were available in 6 1/2 and 8ft lengths. Internal measurements and tailgate dimensions differed between the two box styles as shown in the accompanying chart.

Appearance changes for this year focused on the grille where six rows of

1963 Styleside Pickup Boxes

	Integral		Separate	
Overall box size	6 1/2ft	8ft	61/2ft	8ft
Inside length	78.2in	98.2in	76.2in	94.4in
Inside width	76.6in	76.6in	73.0in	73.0in
Width of tailgate	64.5in	64.5in	51.6in	51.6in
Box height	19.6in	19.6in	19.1in	19.1in

Unlike Chevrolet, which located the distributor at the rear of the engine, Ford gave mechanics doing tune-ups on its V-8 engines an advantage by placing the distributor in the front. On a Ford, all vital engine components can be reached without the mechanic's having to crawl into the engine bay.

short bars that appeared to "float in space" replaced the two long horizontal bars used in 1961 and 1962. Mechanical changes included the new fully synchronized three-speed transmission also offered in cars that year. The fully synchronized three-speed eliminated the awkwardness of trying to match engine rpms to vehicle speed when throwing a downshift to first in busy traffic. Adding to the shifting ease, the clutch and brake pedals were repositioned closer to the floor. On models with the separate Styleside box, the Custom Cab script was mounted on the door.

1964 Trucks

With little fanfare, Ford eliminated the integral cab/box construction on its Styleside pickups. The new separate Styleside boxes had the same load length as before: 6 1/2ft and 8ft in the F-100 and 250 series, and 9ft on the F-350. A center latch replaced the side-mounted latches used on the 1961-1963 Styleside tailgates. With the integral cab/box construction gone, Ford's 4x4 models were now listed with the Styleside box, but although they looked alike from the side, the four-wheel-drive box was very different from the Styleside box used on regular two-wheel-drive pickups. These differences included single-wall construction on the 4x4 box, whereas the regular Styleside box used double wall construction to prevent the outer panels from being damaged by sliding cargo. Also, the 4x4 box used heavier, box-section corners, cross sections that stretched all the way across the bottom of the box, an older-style chain tailgate support, and most noticeably, round, instead of rectangular taillights. The front

1961-63 Integral Cab/ Box Ford Pickups

In 1961, Ford redesigned its pickup trucks. Along with a total styling change that gave the trucks more-rounded lines, the designers made the box and cab one unit on the Styleside models. These trucks were not unit-body construction; the combined box/ cab still rested on a frame. But the entire body was one unit, not two separate pieces as is typically the case with pickups. The integral cab/box concept was not new; the Ranchero used this design and Crosley pickups had also been one-piece construction. What Ford did that others hadn't was apply the integral cab/box design to a truck capable of hauling a good-sized load.

By eliminating the space between the cab and box, Ford's designers added 2in of load space without increasing the truck's overall dimensions; and by making the sides of the box an extension of the cab, they added 3 1/2in in width. This made the new Ford's Styleside box the biggest in its class. These extra inches resulted in an increase of 9 cubic feet in overall capacity for the 8ft box. Besides added load space, the integral Styleside with its new body mounts gave a better ride and reduced noise and vibration levels. Ford also claimed the integral cab/box design increased the rigidity and life of the pickup.

Ford built its one-piece pickup in all three light-truck series: F-100, F-250, and F-350. The standard engine was the 135hp 233ci six. The 160hp 292 V-8 was optional at extra cost. Both engines provided plenty of power and delivered good gas mileage.

Adding to the fuel economy was a high (3.22:1) rear axle, available in the F-100 series only.

Problems with the Integral Cab/Box Design:

This idea worked fine for expanding the box, but the integral design greatly reduced the truck's ability to flex—which is not good for a pickup. Pickups are often overloaded and driven over rough ground, which makes the body and frame twist and distort. In these conditions, pickups with the traditional two-piece cab/box construction are able to handle heavy loads and roll over bumps rather easily. This ability to flex also reduces vibrations and road noise. Also, when an overloaded integral cab/box truck was parked on an uneven surface, say with one wheel in a rut or hole, the doors tended to jam and owners claimed they got stuck inside or couldn't open the doors to get in.

Another problem was rust. Pickup truck boxes rust out because of the abuse they receive and from rain, snow, and road salt. When the box of an integral Styleside rusted, the truck owner couldn't just remove the rusted box and install another one or build a homemade platform bed as could be done with separate cab trucks.

Ford's Solution:

Ford Motor Company had a solution to these problems, but it didn't talk about it very loudly. In 1963 at least (there is some evidence this option was also available as early as 1961), Ford offered a Styleside model using a separate cab and the old wide box from 1957-1960. Although this option is listed in some of Ford's truck ads for 1963, pictures of the truck with the 1957-1960 box are not shown. The truck itself looked like a backyard job because the lines of the 1957-

1960 box and around the wheel cutout are more square and angular then those of 1961-1963.

Today a 1963 Ford truck with a 1957-1960 box is a collector's item. Of course the trick is to determine whether the earlier-style box was installed on the truck at the factory or by a previous owner. In more than a few cases, owners have replaced a rusted out Flareside box on a 1961-1963 Ford with anything that would fit—and the earlier wide Styleside box fits perfectly. However, anyone who is lucky enough to stumble across one of the factory-direct 1963 Fords with the wide 1957-1960 box will have quite a collector's item.

Trim options for the integral cab/box pickups included the Custom cab interior package, which added such dress-up features as a chrome-trimmed instrument cluster, twill stripe upholstery, extra foam padding in the seat, two-tone paint on the dash and doors, and other interior extras.

Popular Mechanics magazine tested a F-100 integral cab/box Styleside pickup in its August 1963 issue. This truck was equipped with the standard 233 six, the medium-duty three-speed, and the standard 3.73:1 rear axle. The truck averaged 18mpg during the testing and had no problem accelerating to highway speeds. The report described the interior as comfortable and spacious, interior noise acceptable, and visibility good. While the turning radius was reported as fairly tight, the writer complained that a strong pair of arms were needed to steer around tight corners. The suspension was described as stiff and solid for hauling purposes—in fact the truck could easily handle a camper and extra weight without bottoming. Overall, *Popular Mechanics* liked the truck and said it was very versatile.

Ford's first solution to problems with the integral cab/box design was to offer the old-style box from the 1957-1960 trucks with the separate cab used on four-wheel-drive and Flareside (fendered box) pickups. There are no records on how many trucks fitted with the older style box were built, and Ford did not play up this option in its advertising.

Original sixties-vintage Ford pickups can still be found hard at work. Hamid Al Ghamdi of Saudi Arabia is restoring this 1966 Ford F-100 that once saw service on an air force base. The dry Saudi climate has preserved this truck's metal, but finding parts for even such basic upgrades as a carburetor rebuild can be a nightmare for many overseas restorers of vintage American cars and trucks.

panel stampings also differ between the two Styleside boxes.

While the short box pickups retained the 114in wheelbase, the longer 8ft bodies in the F-100 and 250 series now rode on a 128in wheelbase (an increase of 6in). The heavy-duty F-350 trucks used a 132in wheelbase, while the 4x4 models continued the 120in chassis. Ford's pickups were growing longer, in part because length was in vogue, but also to make them more adaptable for a variety of uses—especially for toting campers. In 1964, traveling Americans had caught pickup camper fever.

Apart from the separation of cab and box on the Styleside trucks and a slightly longer wheelbase on the 8ft box models, the simplest way to distinguish a 1964 Ford pickup from the three earlier years in this style run is to take a close look at the grille. Although the "floating bars" design from 1963 had been carried over, there were now four rows of bars instead of six. Not only were the bars wider, they were also fatter and enclosed a rectangular opening. In addition to this difference in grille design,

the Ford lettering on top of the grille was spaced wider apart.

Engine choices were expanded for 1964 to include an optional 262ci six. The new six retained the fuel economy for which six-cylinder engines have been noted, but gave increased torque for more heavy duty work. By 1964, Ford-O-Matic had been dropped from the transmission list, replaced by heavy-duty Cruise-O-Matic, even on the F-100. Customers who ordered the 262 six found themselves limited in transmission options since neither overdrive nor automatic was available with that engine. A limited slip differential could be specified in any of the five available rear axle ratios: 3.89:1 (standard), plus 3.70, 4.11, 3.73, 3.92, and 4.10.

By the mid-sixties, designers were giving serious attention to truck interiors, and the new Fords were no exception. The Custom cab now featured color-keyed interiors including upholstery, steering wheel and column, and even a color-coordinated floor mat. Door panels were also color-matched with contrasting (white) inserts. The instrument panel, too, was painted in a matching two-color scheme. Door steps were covered with aluminum scuff plates and bright metal was used to decorate the instrument cluster. The acoustical headliner now extended down to the beltline in the rear quarters and was held in place by bright metal moldings. Included, too, were a storage compartment in the left door, cigar lighter, right-side sun visor, extra foam padding in the seat and back-

rest, as well as the Custom Cab emblem on each door.

Ford designed its light trucks to fit the customer's job or purpose. Counting the compact Econoline, Ranchero, and standard pickups, buyers could select from sixteen different models. In addition, Ford's standard pickup could be ordered as a bare chassis-cab and combined with aftermarket utility bodies that gave contractors, plumbers, and other tradespeople storage room to haul tools and supplies. With a snowplow blade up front and wrecker boom installed in the pickup box, Ford's four-wheel-drive light trucks became all-around road service vehicles. Travelers wishing to take the comforts of home with them could select from a number of camper bodies, some that fit into the pickup box, others that mounted directly on the chassis.

Although the remaining three years in the model series would carry the same styling, 1964 marked the end of an era for Ford's light trucks. It would be the last year of the rigid front axle that had originated with the buggy. Pickup sales were climbing every year. In 1964, Ford was nudging the half-million mark with 458,583 light trucks produced. Independent front suspension would be the breakthrough that would push sales over 500,000.

1965 Trucks

Although a new grille and repositioned parking lights identified Ford's new trucks, big changes could be found underneath the hood, plus there was the all-new front suspension. Ford engineers had created not one, but three new engines: two sixes and a V-8. The standard six displaced 240ci and developed 150hp at 4000rpm. The optional "Big Six" displaced 300ci and produced 170hp. The new V-8 now displaced 352ci and was rated at 208hp. Both sixes featured seven main bearing crankshafts and hydraulic valve lifters for longer life and quieter operation. The 352 V-8, a ruggedly reliable engine, would become a mainstay in the Ford stable.

Most years, new engines would have been the most talked about feature, but for 1965, Ford chose to focus buyer's attention on the new (for Ford) independent front suspension. When Chevrolet, GMC, and International made the breakthrough from rigid front axles to independent suspension, all three adopted a rugged torsion bar arrangement linked to independent A arms. In Chevrolet and GMC's case, the torsion bars were extended even to the big trucks. On the light trucks, the Chevy/GMC independent front end design required a massively reinforced frame, adding weight and cost. As a result, although Chevrolet and GMC retained independent front suspension (IFS) on their light trucks, they dropped the torsion bar design in 1963 and substituted a coil spring arrangement that appeared very similar to that found on Chevrolet cars; in fact some parts interchanged. International also eventually abandoned torsion bar front suspension, returning to a beam front axle. In designing its independent front suspension, Ford was determined to create a rugged front end that wouldn't require expensive frame modification. The result became "Twin I Beam" suspension.

In creating the Twin I Beam arrangement Ford's engineers retained the basic engineering of an old-fashioned beam axle, added coil springs, and, with a bit of cluging, created a rugged, relatively cheap to build, independently sprung front end that gave the desired car-like ride. Here's how they did it. First, the traditional king pins were retained at each wheel, but rather than attaching both wheels to a single axle, each wheel had its own axle stub. The axle stubs both ran underneath the frame and anchored to mounting brackets on the bottom of the opposing frame channel. To prevent forward or backward movement, each axle stub was held in place by a rugged, forged steel radius rod (similar to the radius rods used on Ford's buggy-style front ends of the Model T, A, and early V-8 eras). Coil springs perched atop the radius rod/axle juncture, held in place by frame brackets. Twin I Beam design is at the same time simpler (it really represents only the most reluctant departure from a solid front end) and more complex (in the sense that it uses more parts) than a conventional A-arm

The interior of this 1965 Ford pickup has a plain, almost stark, appearance. Through the mid-sixties, manufacturers still thought of light trucks primarily as working vehicles. This image would soon change, however, leading to truck interiors every bit as luxurious as a car's.

To provide safe storage for tools and other small items, Ford offered this "hideaway" stowage box, mounted in the outside of the pickup bed on the passenger side, as an extra-cost option.

and coil spring passenger car (and Chevy/GMC light truck) solution to independent front suspension.

Twin I Beam suspension delivered what it promised, as is proven by the fact that it is still in use thirty years later. Ford's light trucks could now compete

Opening the box's cover revealed two storage cavities. Unfortunately, the easily "jimmied" lock wasn't much of a challenge for a serious thief.

with Chevrolet for a silky ride, even over washboard-rough roads. The new suspension spurred sales and Ford crossed the half-million mark with its light truck production for 1965, totaling 563,137.

Inside the cab, the emphasis was on comfort once again. A vinyl floor mat replaced the former rubber mats for greater durability. Interior colors now included red, blue, green, or beige, color-keyed to the exterior. Air conditioning was available as were two heater options.

Also new for 1965 were Camper Special packages in both the F-100 and 250 series. The Camper Special on the F-100 used a 129in wheelbase, the "Big Six" or V-8 engine, heavy-duty front springs, an extra-capacity radiator and alternator, heavy-duty battery, extended tail pipe, oil pressure gauge and ammeter, plus West Coast sideview mirrors. Two camper packages could be selected in the F-250 series: a "custom" or "deluxe." Both used the 129in wheelbase and other features of the F-100 Camper Special, but added heavier duty 2400lb rating rear springs and a 4.10 rear axle (either standard or limited slip). The difference between the F-250 custom and deluxe camper packages is seen mainly in cab and trim upgrades, which on the deluxe included padded dash and visors, seat belts, chrome front bumper, two-tone paint and body side moldings, and right-side tool storage box built into the pickup body. The Camper Specials carried a special insignia on the front quarter panel just below the beltline molding.

1966 Trucks

Ford's light truck focus for 1966 remained on comfort and style. Twin I Beam front suspension gave a passenger car smooth ride, and interior offerings were the plushest yet. Although the body was now six years old, the style still didn't look especially dated. The easiest way to distinguish the 1966 models from their predecessors is by the grille, which now featured a horizontal bar and twin spear-shaped openings above two rows of small rectangular cutouts. This grille is busier than 1965. Bigger differences are found inside the cab.

"Drab cabs are out," Ford sales brochures for 1966 proclaimed. Whether the buyer ordered the standard or Custom cab, interior color schemes ranged from red to blue, green or beige—all color-keyed to the exterior finish. On Custom cabs, even the floor mat was color coordinated. Door locks were now fitted to both doors, even on the standard cab. The Custom cab featured woven seat covering for greater comfort in hot weather. A new deluxe Ranger option included bucket seats color-keyed in red, palomino, beige, or black, and an additional cost center console, plus floor carpeting. Trucks equipped with the Ranger dress-up package are identified with a "Ranger" emblem.

On November 1, 1965, power steering became an option on all Ford light trucks. Power brakes were also included on the option list for the F-100 and 250 models. Though not a frequently purchased pickup option, white sidewall tires could also be specified. The three camper packages introduced in 1965 were continued in 1966.

By 1966, Ford had a product for every corner of the light truck market, starting with the light-duty Econoline and car/pickup Ranchero, extending through the F-100, 250, and rugged 350 models—with four-wheel-drive offered in both the F-100 and 250 series—and now including the all-new Bronco utility 4x4. Even so, sales dropped slightly to 553,719.

Of significance, Ford (like Chevy and GMC) was now producing trucks that could double for a car in comfort and interior appointments. With the camper craze and utility four-wheel-drive market extending beyond hunters and ranchers, middle class, suburban households were finding it stylish, and practical, to have a light truck parked in the driveway. Americans were developing a taste for light trucks—a phenomenon that would build for the next two decades.

Chapter 11

1967-1979: Positioning for Number One

After a six-year run, Ford's truck line had again grown dated, so new styling appeared in 1967, which also turned out to be a new-look year for Chevy. The new trucks at Ford and Chevy dealerships clearly came from different drawing boards. Through the early sixties, trucks carrying GM nameplates had worn a boxy styling, whereas the new 1967 models adopted a softer, more angled look. At Ford, the reverse styling sequence occurred. The previous models had worn the softer, more rounded styling, while the new 1967 models received a sharp, crisp look that had the twin benefits of appearing functional while avoiding following styling fads. The crisp look wore well, lasting with only minor revisions through 1979. Actually, Ford truck styling through the early nineties represents only a mild refinement of the new look presented by the 1967 models. Chevy, in contrast, completely abandoned its 1967 styling in 1973.

Through aggressive product development, Ford now covered every niche of the light truck market. For the sport truck buyer, there was the Ranchero; Econoline vans and pickups fit the bill for those concerned about size and oper-

In 1970, Ford pickups adopted a split grille design that continued as a Ford truck "trademark" through 1977.

ating economy; the Bronco stood alone as a driver-friendly vehicle for the off-road utility 4x4 set; and Ford's new full-size pickups in both two- and four-wheel-drive versions, available with six- or eight-cylinder engines in load ratings of half-, three-quarter-and one-ton filled practically all other light-duty hauling needs. By the mid-sixties light truck sales had begun their upward climb that

In 1970, Ford introduced the upscale Ranger pickup series. Externally, this package included added bright roof rails and rear window molding, rocker panel and wheel lip moldings, and a decorative tailgate panel.

would eventually put light trucks ahead of cars on the sales charts—and Ford trucks were at the top of the charts. For the ensuing sales battle Ford had positioned itself well with a product lineup no other truck manufacturer could match.

Although no one would mistake a 1967 or later Ford truck as anything but a Ford, there is little connection in styling between the 1967 pickups and Ford's earlier trucks. The curved windshield replaced the semi-wrap-around windshield seen in the 1961-1966 series trucks. Gone, too, were the sweeps at the rear of the wheel housings. Wider cabs with more deluxe interior appointments further reduced the comfort difference between driving or riding in a car and a new Ford truck while seat upholstery and interior coverings color-keyed to the exterior replaced the drab interiors once expected in a truck.

Less visible than appearance changes and perhaps less appreciated than improvements in comfort were the major safety advances in the 1967 trucks. A dual hydraulic braking system now provided stopping power should a brake line rupture or a wheel cylinder fail. A warning light monitored brake fluid level, alerting the operator to severe brake lining wear or fluid loss. Standard safety equipment also included seat belts and emergency flashers. Mechanically,

When Ford restyled its pickups in 1967, it returned to the squared off look of its late sixties trucks. This crisp look has worn well, serving as the styling trademark of Ford trucks into the nineties.

the most notable advance for 1967 came in Ford's extending its Twin I Beam front suspension to the F-350 series trucks.

Engine and drivetrain specifications remained the same as 1966 with the 240ci, 150hp six standard and a 300ci, 170hp six or 352ci, 208hp V-8 optional. In the more recent years of this styling series, Ford's 302 V-8, along with the 360, 390, and 460 V-8s, joined the engine listing, with the 351 and 400ci engines later replacing the 360 and 460 versions. Transmission options included the standard three-speed, three-speed and overdrive, four-speed, or Cruise-O-Matic. By 1967, Ford was the only manufacturer still offering the engine-saving, gas

Previous page
The crisp look that Ford introduced in 1967 wore well, lasting with only minor changes through 1979. The 1970 Ranger model shown here is owned by Wilber Bergman of Thomasboro, Illinois.

mileage-boosting three-speed and overdrive transmission combination. According to the option sheets, overdrive continued to be available on Ford's F-100 models through 1970, though finding a truck so equipped would be unusual indeed. Desirable and beneficial as an overdrive transmission is, the manually controlled Borg-Warner overdrive units fell out of popularity in the mid-fifties with the advent of more powerful V-8 engines and automatic transmissions.

For contractors and others needing a pickup that could double as a transport vehicle, Ford added a six-man crew cab model in its F-250 and F-350 series. And for those who really worked their trucks, Ford still built plain-jane models with durable black vinyl interiors. But with truck popularity on the rise, Ford's truck marketing emphasis shifted to upscale models equipped with bucket seats, power steering, and air conditioning as well as dress-up trim packages. Over the thirteen years of this styling series, model year updates are visible mainly in grille treatment with a divided grille appearing in 1970 and continuing with variations to the grid design until 1978, when Ford trucks adopted the egg-crate grille design popularized by Chevrolet in 1955. A minor styling revision occurred in 1973 when Ford's Styleside (wide bed)

On its pickups, Ford set the side marker lights, federally mandated in 1968, attractively into the series emblems.

pickups acquired a front-to-rear crease at the location of the side trim spear.

In 1974 Ford introduced its popular SuperCab, which allowed a family with small children to travel together in a pickup. SuperCabs could be ordered with one of two rear seating arrangements: a narrow, full-width bench seat that could be folded down to provide inside storage space behind the front seat, or a pair of inward facing jump seats. While the back seat area of a SuperCab pickup can't be described as roomy, this model did make it possible for young families to purchase a pickup as their primary vehicle.

With half-ton pickups falling under the same antipollution equipment requirements as cars, in 1974 Ford made a very clever move by marketing a line of heavy-duty half-ton models, designated the F-150 series, that were exempt from catalytic converters and other hardware that most truckers considered a nuisance. As an added bonus, standard equipment in the F-150 models was Ford's 300ci six. Along with a somewhat beefier suspension and the absence of the antipollution equipment, standard

power brakes distinguished the F-150 models from their F-100 cousins.

Besides the SuperCab and F-150, developments to Ford's full-size pickups through the seventies consisted mainly of a variety of special trim and equipment packages. These included the posh Ranger XLT, introduced in 1970, as well as the upscale Explorer package, which first appeared in 1971. Once the public had tasted deluxe trucks with their added soundproofing and more car-like interiors, demand for the fancier trucks led Ford marketers to expand the special package offerings. In 1972 writing the words *Northland Package* on the order form brought truck buyers living in colder climates a truck with factory-equipped engine block heater, heavy-

duty battery, and traction lock rear axle. The pickup camper craze also led Ford to offer camper special models equipped with heavy-duty front and rear stabilizer bars, larger-output alternators, western-style sideview mirrors, extra-capacity cooling systems, and high-output V-8 engines. No longer were pickup trucks marketed on the "one style fits all" philosophy.

The Econoline pickup made its last appearance in the 1967 lineup, leaving Ford without an entry in the compact pickup field. Rather than design a new small pickup from the ground up, Ford chose to import a mini pickup built by Mazda and market it under the Courier nameplate. A divided grid-pattern grille gave this small truck a Ford look.

Inside the cab, the Ranger comfort and convenience package included wood grain inserts in the instrument cluster, pleated vinyl door trim with simulated wood grain inserts and bright molding around the arm rests, pleated cloth and vinyl upholstery, color-keyed carpeting, plus extra insulation and sound deadening.

Through 1978, Ford Courier pickups used a 109.5ci four-cylinder, overhead cam engine rated at 74hp coupled to a four-speed transmission. In 1979, a larger, more powerful 120ci engine rated at 77hp became standard, and transmission options included an automatic or five-speed manual. The Courier carried the Ford nameplate well and filled the compact pickup slot in Ford's truck lineup until replaced by the home-grown

The Ranger dress-up package also included stylish full-wheel covers.

Ranger pickup in 1982.

Through the seventies, Ford continued to fall short of the number one sales position held by Chevrolet, but its well-built, smartly styled trucks aimed at just about every market niche were closing the gap. By the end of the next decade, Ford would pull ahead in the fierce sales competition that placed the pickup truck in the center of many Americans' lives.

By the seventies, the modern pickup had evolved.

You can justifiably wonder how many of today's pickup trucks really get used for work.
Pickups had become so well-accepted as daily
transportation in the nineties that special
models were developed, such as the Splash
shown here. A customized Ranger pickup, the
Splash was created for a buyer who was under 30, wanted a colorful and sporty pickup,
and had annual median income of close to
$30,000. Note there's no mention of that buy-
er's hauling needs. Ford estimated that 40
percent of all Splash buyers would be women.
Ford Motor Company

Chapter 12

The Eighties and Nineties:
Ford Trucks Top the Sales Charts

The restyling that occurred for 1980 is so mild and subtle that unless a 1979 or earlier and 1980 or later Ford truck are parked side-by-side, it's easy to miss the fundamental changes that occurred. What this says is that evolutionary changes sometimes make a stronger statement and have more appeal than drastic changes. Rather than softening the squarish styling of the 1979 and earlier models, Ford's 1980 and newer full-size trucks have an even crisper look, seen most prominently in the angled corner at the rear of the cab as well a similarly angled opening at the rear of the doors. Taller side windows that dip below the base of the windshield as well as a taller windshield that now blends with the forward edge of the cab roof mark the remaining, most visible changes. Of significance to the driver, the interiors of Ford's most current light-duty trucks have become increasingly posh with cloth upholstery, optional bucket seats, and car-like ergonomics that include power windows and door locks as well as sound systems that match the quality of the musical equipment found in premium motor cars.

Along with styling and interior comfort, Ford's light-duty trucks owe their sales success to a model lineup that fills every market niche. Starting with the full-size F-series, Ford's current truck line includes wide-bodied Styleside as well as traditional narrow box Flareside pickups in short or long wheelbase configurations; extra seat SuperCab models as well as the traditional single seat cab; and four- as well as two-wheel drive. During the eighties, the most significant engineering advances came through new applications for electronics—including electronically controlled fuel injection, which, by the nineties, could be found on all Ford light-duty truck engines, four-cylinder, V-6, and V-8; and Electric Touch Drive for the 4x4 models. Traditionally, the hassle with four-wheel-drive has been that either the front drive hubs are engaged constantly, greatly increasing unnecessary wear to the front driveline and decreasing fuel mileage, or the operator has to stop the truck and manually engage the front drive hubs before venturing into treacherous terrain. The problem with manually engaging the front hubs is that the driver can't always predict when road or off-road conditions will require the traction of four-wheel-drive. On Ford trucks equipped with Electronic Touch Drive, the operator simply presses the 4x4 button on the dash and electronics do the rest. The truck doesn't need to be stopped or even slowed down for the front drive system to engage. Likewise, the driver can shift back to

two-wheel-drive at the press of a button.

The eighties also saw significant advances in fuel economy, with gains achieved partly through electronic fuel injection, but also due to four- or five-speed overdrive transmissions and higher (lower numerical) gear ratios. The combination of improved fuel mileage and high-capacity fuel tanks enables the most current Ford full-size trucks to provide nearly a full day's driving on a single fill-up. Other advances include six-year, 100,000-mile corrosion protection and vibrant paint colors, protected and given greater depth of gloss by clear coat finishes.

Since 1966 Ford's 4x2 full-size light-duty trucks have used a unique Twin I Beam independent front suspension that has earned a reputation for combining the smooth ride of a car with the toughness and durability of a truck. Full-size Ford trucks have also continued to offer V-8 power, giving them stamina for towing trailers and carrying heavy loads.

Ford has long recognized that many truck admirers don't need the hauling capacity of a full-size pickup. Beginning with the Econoline pickup, then the Mazda-built Courier, and more recently the Ranger mini pickup, Ford's light-duty truck line has included junior, as well as senior-sized trucks. Through 1982, the Mazda-built Courier compact

Drivers who wanted the look and style of a pickup with the performance of a Mustang could opt for the 1993 F150 Lightning model. The Lightning came from Ford's Special Vehicle Team, and is an example of modern-day pickup buyers' interest in the look, style, and image of a truck as their daily driver. In the case of the Lightning, they also get plenty of performance. In the old days, 0-60mph times weren't critical to pickup buyers, but times—and the pickup market—have changed. Ford Motor Company

pickup served as Ford's down-sized pickup offering. Although the Courier shared a styling resemblance with the full-sized trucks and had earned a reputation for durability, a fully-Ford replacement—fittingly named the Ranger, which was formerly the name used for Ford's top-of-

the-line full-sized truck—replaced the Courier in 1982.

Visually, the compact Ranger pickup is the spitting image of its full-size brother. The cab wears the same crisp angular lines. Grille treatment, side sculpting, and rear light design also match the big trucks. Besides the Ranger's junior size, the other distinguishing visual feature between Ford's maxi- and mini pickups is the absence of vent windows on the Ranger. Its trimmer weight and lower profile enable the mini truck to slip through the wind more easily, and Rangers are fitted with V-4 or V-6 engines that also have multiport electronic fuel injection. As with the big pickups, Rangers are offered in regular or SuperCab styles with interiors equally as posh as the full-size trucks and every bit as comfortable as a car.

Rangers can be fitted with four-wheel-drive and also carry the Electronic Touch Drive feature, which enables drivers to engage or disengage the front-drive hubs with a push of a button on the instrument panel. For versatility over a wide range of driving conditions and also to improve fuel economy, Ranger buyers can specify five-speed with overdrive manual or automatic transmissions.

With the 1980 styling update, Ford also reworked the Bronco, which it slimmed down modestly to eliminate excess bulk and improve agility and fuel economy. The new Bronco shared all front clip parts and overall styling with the full-size pickups. Buyers looking to combine the utility of a truck with the comfort of a car could specify pile carpeting and cloth seats while a variety of exterior dress-up, suspension, and engine packages were available for those who wanted to set their utility vehicle apart from the crowd or outfit it for towing or other special use purposes. In 1984, the Bronco II joined Ford's light-duty 4x4 lineup. As with the Ranger, the Bronco II was a downsized copy of the full-sized Bronco. A V-6 engine supplied the Bronco II's power needs and delivered good fuel economy.

In recent years, the hottest item in the compact utility market has been Ford's four-door Explorer. This vehicle, which combines styling features and passenger capacity of a van with the traction and off-road capability of a 4x4 utility, became an instant sales success. Attractive styling and interiors designed for driver and passenger comfort as well as aesthetic appeal are also factors in the Explorer's popularity. Powertrain combinations fit Ford's multiport fuel-injected V-6 with a four-speed automatic or five-speed manual transmission.

The automotive press has lavished praise on the Explorer for its style, performance, and roomy interior, describing Ford's newest compact utility as the perfect family vehicle. With 42.6 cubic feet of cargo space behind the rear seats, an Explorer is an ideal vehicle for families on vacation. The four doors allow easy access to the rear seat, something lacking in earlier Broncos and Bronco IIs. (Besides the four door model, Ford also builds a two-door Explorer that more closely resembles its Bronco predecessor.) As an added convenience, the rear storage area can be accessed either by raising the liftgate or by opening just the liftgate's window. The Explorer contains several other design pluses, including a spare tire that stows between rear frame rails but lowers with crank mechanism, and engineering advances such as antilock brakes. With the Explorer, Ford created an all-purpose winner.

Vans complete the Ford light-duty truck lineup. In 1984, the Aerostar, a compact van whose styling drew inspiration from America's space shuttles, joined the full-size Club Wagon. Like Ford's other downsized trucks, the Aerostar uses V-6 power.

For 1992 the Club Wagon received a major restyle that softened the body lines and upgraded the interior with car-like luxury. Like the Explorer, the Club Wagon has been highly praised. *Motor Trend* magazine selected Ford's Club Wagon as its 1992 Truck of the Year. In its tribute, *Motor Trend* wrote: "Since this Club Wagon is the first all-new full-size van in 17 years, Ford could have done a mild revamp and it still would have been leagues ahead of the competition. Instead, Ford decided to do it right, investing $1.2 billion into development and tooling—an effort well spent... Ford did a first rate job of not only bringing the full-size van into the '90s, but in creating a new standard in comfortable people movers."

Indeed, *Motor Trend*'s observations capture not just the success of the Club Wagon but the reason behind Ford's success in achieving the number one position on America's light truck sales charts. Ford Motor Company's Truck Division has invested heavily and wisely in new designs that are useful and a pleasure to drive, and in engineering that combines performance with economy and reliability. With success in its hands, Ford didn't rest on its laurels. In the extremely competitive light truck arena, future offerings must exceed the current all-star cast, not just in serving buyers' needs, but also by firing their excitement.

With the Econoline, Ford created a compact, fuel efficient, highly versatile "cab forward" pickup. This design was so successful that Dodge copied it nearly intact for its A-100.

Chapter 13

Econoline:
Lots of Truck in a Small Package

Ford introduced the Econoline compact van and pickup series in October 1960 to compete with Volkswagen's transporter vehicles. Body styles of the new Ford commercial line included a bus (window van), van, and pickup. Powered by the new Falcon-based 144ci six, these small trucks met the two marketing criteria needed to compete with Volkswagen: economy and versatile light hauling. The Econoline pickup's 7ft box with tall, 22.8in sides gave more cargo room for bulky loads than Volkswagen pickups. With width dimensions at the tailgate and wheel housing measuring 49in and 48in, respectively, the Econoline could easily carry 4x8 sheets of plywood and other building materials. Load capacity was limited by payload rating more than cargo capacity. Lacking a separate frame, the Econoline was nominally rated at one-half-ton and limited to a 1650lb payload.

The Econoline's cab-forward design with its large windows gave the compact truck excellent maneuverability, and although sitting at the very front of a vehicle takes some getting used to, vision (particularly in cabs that were fitted with rear quarter windows) was virtually unobstructed. As with other light trucks of the era, some attempt was made to provide an appealing interior, and to this end Ford used a durable yet mildly stylish brown vinyl seat covering with basket-weave inserts.

To protect the outer sheet metal and preserve the structural integrity of the unit-body, the rocker panels and all under-body support members were zinc coated prior to painting. Suspension members on this traditionally designed compact truck included an I Beam axle with leaf springs up front and a differential plus leaf springs in the rear. The only departures from mechanical features that could be found on any light truck were the in-cab engine location and front shock absorber mounting points that were placed high in the wheel wells.

To give its new Econoline pickups wider appeal, Ford offered a Custom Equipment package that included a right-hand ventilation duct, armrests, cigarette lighter, driver's side door lock, chrome horn ring, dual horns, bright metal hub caps, extra foam padding for the seat, a right hand sun visor, and a passenger seat.

Along with filling a wide range of light hauling functions for delivery services and the like, Econolines were also purchased in large numbers by the military as light-duty transport vehicles, and they saw service both domestically and abroad. The little trucks were fun to drive, though they were somewhat treacherous on loose gravel roads as the unloaded rear end could break loose without warning on decreasing radius turns. Production continued through 1967, with fancier options and additional engines appearing along the way.

1961 Econolines

Early Econolines were intended as no-frills delivery vehicles and consequently had few luxury or convenience features. Most had no radio or heater and many had only a driver's seat—although some were equipped with a swing-away passenger seat. Many had only a single sun visor, no armrests, and some even came without an outside lock on the driver's door. Options such as cab insulation, a padded dash, and a glovebox door could be ordered, but few of the early vehicles came with these extras. All of the 1961s were fitted with the 144ci engine and three-speed transmission, which was not synchronized into first gear.

1962 Econolines

In 1962 the big news was the optional 170ci six-cylinder engine. Reinforcing ribs were added to the roof of the vans at midyear to prevent the annoying drumming of the roof metal at highway speeds. Also added was a Deluxe Club Wagon package for the Falcon window vans. This was a fancy trim package that included Viking Blue metallic paint, out-

The driver's position at the front of the truck makes an Econoline highly maneuverable and fun to drive. The optional five-window cab gave excellent visibility and the 90hp, 144ci six pushed the light truck along easily at highway speeds while delivering up to 27mpg.

side trim strips with anodized inserts that ran the length of the body, chrome bumpers, vinyl front door panels, a blue padded dash and glovebox door, full headliner, floor mats, and upholstered side panels for the rear seating area.

1963 Econolines

Several new features were offered in 1963. Most notable was the heavy duty three-speed transmission, which was fully synchronized in all forward gears. An eight-door van was introduced this year that had cargo doors on both sides. The front turn signal lenses, which had

previously been clear, were now amber. Midyear options included the British-built Dagenham four-speed transmission with column shift and a heavy-duty package consisting of the 170 engine, heavy-duty rear axle, stiffer springs, reinforced frame, and 14in wheels.

1964 Econolines

There were few changes in 1964. Self-adjusting brakes were now standard; the vent windows had locking buttons; a panel van with no side doors was now available; an automatic transmission was included in the option list; and an alternator could be ordered in place of the generator.

1965 Econolines

The Econoline series saw major changes in 1965. The Supervan appeared with an extra 18in of body length behind the rear wheels. The Supervan could be ordered with or without win-

dows in all trim levels, and it had rectangular taillights instead of the round ones used on the short vans. Two new engines were offered: the 200 and 240ci sixes. The 144 six was discontinued, as was the four-speed transmission. Starting this year, the engine was mounted on a tubular cross-member instead of the former cantilever arms. The new bumpers were thicker and stronger; on vans, the license plate was relocated from the bumper to the left cargo door; the heater was moved from the floor to the right side air vent; and air flow was regulated by cable controls on the dash. The seats sat lower and were better padded; an optional instrumentation package replaced the oil and alternator warning lights with gauges; and an alternator was now standard. A deluxe pickup was introduced, and it was painted only in Poppy Red and used the Deluxe Club Wagon's outside trim and chrome bumpers.

1966 Econolines

Few changes were made in 1966. Emergency flashers, previously optional, were now standard. The padded dash and glovebox became standard in midyear, and a push-button lock was added to the padded glovebox door.

1967 Econolines

In 1967 several changes occurred. For instance, the dual hydraulic brake system mandated by federal law was adopted. This included a warning lamp above the headlight switch to indicate a loss of pressure in part of the system. Two-speed wipers were now standard; they had been optional since 1961. Backup lamps also became standard equipment; previously, backup lamps had not been available even as an option. The emergency flasher switch was moved to the steering column as part of the turn signal switch, and the automatic transmission shift pattern changed from P-R-N-D2-D1-L to P-R-N-D-2-1.

1968 Econolines

The 1967 models continued unchanged into the first part of the 1968 model year and were sold as 1967 models. In mid-1968 the new engine-forward vans were introduced as 1969 models and the Econoline pickup was discontinued.

Econoline Driving Impressions
by Jay B. Long

The Econoline van and pickup were originally designed as basic, no-frills delivery and work trucks. They were intended to be compact, economical vehicles that would compete with Volkswagen's Transporter series. The resulting vehicles more than accomplished their goals and were copied almost exactly by the Dodge A-100 series and the vans offered by Chevrolet/GMC a few years later.

The earliest Econolines were very basic in nature. All were equipped with a small six-cylinder engine and manual gearbox. The interiors were plain and functional, and not much more. Few had any options. The few options available were things that are taken for granted on new vehicles today: a radio, heater, padded dash, sun visors, armrests, and even the passenger seat. The outside lock on the driver's side cost extra also, as did the cardboard insulation on the front of the body.

Despite the lack of amenities, the Econoline is surprisingly comfortable to drive. The seating position is directly above the front wheels. In fact, the seats are bolted directly to the wheel wells. The engine is between the front seats, slightly behind the front axle. All of the controls are within easy reach and feel natural to operate. The gearshift is on the steering column, with long but easy throws. The seating position is upright, and there is a lot of legroom and headroom, even for a tall person. The steering wheel is nearly horizontal but feels comfortable after a few minutes behind the wheel. Steering is quick and light, despite the lack of power assist.

The Econoline is extremely maneuverable due to its short wheelbase and mid-engine weight distribution. The ride is firm, but not excessively harsh. With the forward seating position, judging a turn takes a bit of getting used to, but visibility is excellent. The gearing on the early models makes freeway driving a bit noisy since the engine is giving its all at 55mph, but the later models with a bigger engine have taller gearing and can be driven all day at 70. Engine noise and heat are surprisingly low, considering the engine is right next to the driver. The wind noise varies from moderate to quite a lot, depending on whether there is a headwind or tailwind. Stability at speed is good; you can feel the wind and road surface but the vehicle never feels unmanageable. Handling is neutral up to the point where all four wheels break loose. The problem to avoid here is hitting the brakes hard and locking the rear wheels, because if you do so, the truck is likely to end up on its side. With no load in the rear the rear wheels will lock up well before the fronts. The brakes are good for one panic stop from 70mph, but not much more, so on a long downgrade the truck should be controlled by wind resistance or gearing. Economy varies from extremely good (up to 27mpg with the small six) to fair (16mpg with the big six used for freeway driving). Maintenance and repairs are simple and can be performed without jacking the wheels off the ground. Reliability is top notch, as all mechanical systems are conventional and have been proven on trucks for years.

All in all, Econolines are fun and practical vehicles to drive. They are safe and comfortable when driven as they were intended to be, and they have the distinction of being the first American compact vans and pickups.

Chapter 14

Bronco:
Taming the Wild Frontier

From 1960-1965, the four-wheel-drive sport-utility vehicle market grew in annual sales from 11,000 to 35,000 vehicles, more than a three-fold increase in just five years. The introduction of International's popular Scout in 1961 gave the sport-utility vehicle market its biggest boost since Willys had offered the war jeep in civilian dress at the end of World War II. Although Scouts and jeeps may come to mind first as the early entries in the utility vehicle market, by the midsixties Land Rover, Datsun Patrol, and Toyota Land Cruiser were also making a bid for a share of the four-wheel-drive utility vehicle market.

Ford's first small 4x4 since its World War II jeep wasn't a quickly conceived response to a growing market. Rather, the Bronco was based on meticulous marketing research. In planning the Bronco, Ford researchers had talked with members of 300 off-road clubs. In a research survey that went out to more than 10,000 four-wheel-drive buffs, Ford's designers learned what these "drive 'em to the fringe of nowhere" people wanted. Tops on their list were qualities like comfort, good ride, versatility,

With the Bronco, Ford created a comfortable, go-anywhere vehicle whose styling, though basically functional, had a "let's go have some fun" look about it.

As an alternative to the standard 170ci, Bronco buyers in 1971 could option Ford's popular 302ci V-8. Truck's so-equipped wore the 302 emblems seen here above the side marker lights on the front fenders.

and good handling, but their wish list also included higher cruising speeds, weather-tight cabs, a shorter turning radius, softer seats, and a convenient network of parts and service dealerships. With this list in hand, Ford's engineers set out to fill the bill.

The Bronco was all the 4x4 buffs had asked for—and more. Wider and more car-like than a jeep, with softer suspension and the power to be quicker down the road than a Scout, the Bronco packaged the Falcon 170ci six-cylinder engine, Mustang bucket seats, coil spring front suspension, and a rugged ladder frame into a good-looking, comfortable, off-road utility vehicle.

I had the pleasure of borrowing a friend's 1966 Bronco for a few days one summer some years back. Its soft top had been removed when my wife, our then-small boys, and I picked it up, so we enjoyed full panoramic views, sunshine, and wind whipping our clothing as we romped the hills and mountain paths around our home in rural Vermont. This little Ford utility was equally at home on the highway or off-road. It could cruise to town comfortably at the then-legal highway speeds of 60mph and above. Off-road, the deep coil springs let the wheels roll smoothly over rocks and ruts. Its bucket seats held my wife and me in sports car comfort and the bench seat in the rear gave our kids their own

private perch. We didn't go so far as to fold the windshield down onto the hood for bugs-in-the-teeth motoring, but we sure enjoyed the outdoors in a way we hadn't before.

Although the Bronco looked much wider than a Scout, the actual variation was only .2in (with the Bronco measuring 68.8in wide compared to 68.6in for the Scout). Similarly, the Bronco looked shorter that the Scout, but again the measurements are nearly identical (a 152.1in overall length for the Bronco compared to 154in for the Scout). Height, too, seemed disproportionate, with the Bronco looking several inches higher, but again, the difference is minimal (69.2in for the Bronco and 68in for the Scout). Clearly, nearly identical dimensions did not result in similar-looking vehicles. One of the reasons that the Bronco looked shorter than the Scout was its shorter wheelbase (92in for the Bronco compared to 100in on the Scout). The squared-off lines helped identify the Bronco as a Ford product. There's even a taste of Mustang (as least to my eye) in a Bronco profile.

Along with the basic open vehicle (which could be fitted with a soft top), the Bronco could be ordered with either a short metal top covering just the front seats and giving an open pickup box in the back, or with a full steel top. Most Broncos had the full top, which could be removed easily by loosening a few bolts. The soft top didn't fold down; it also lifted off.

Bronco powertrain elements, except the transfer case and front differential, were a combination of Ford car and light-truck items. The standard three-speed transmission with synchromesh in all forward gears was a real plus in a vehicle where the ability to throw a smooth, quick shift from second to first could mean maintaining momentum to climb that ridge or traverse a bog. Although the Bronco used a stiff front axle, the heavy-duty radius rods and the coil spring arrangement closely resembled the Twin I Beam layout that had been newly adapted to Ford's pickups. The coil

One of the Bronco's most appealing features was the full cap that gave the comfort of a station wagon but could be removed to give the open-air feel of a sporty runabout. The 1971 Bronco shown here is owned by Allen and Pat Gephardt of Washington, Missouri.

Ford selected the Bronco name to capture the sporty image established by its highly popular Mustang.

front suspension not only gave a softer ride than Bronco's competitors, but also a tighter turning radius. The Bronco required only 33.6ft to negotiate a complete circle, compared with 38ft for the Scout. The standard 4.11:1 rear axle ratio represented a compromise between highway speed and climbing power. For those who needed to maximize power at the expense of speed, a 4.57 rear axle was available.

Noise, which had been a complaint of Scouts and jeeps, was pleasantly absent in the Bronco due to a well-insulated steel body and silent transfer case. The only fault road testers could find with Ford's little 4x4 was the absence of the gutsy 289 V-8 engine and an automatic transmission. In response to this criticism, Ford made the 289 V-8 rated at 200hp an option at midyear 1966.

The "endless option" policy that had found such success on the Mustang also applied to the Bronco. Included were twin fuel tanks (the primary fuel tank had a 14gal capacity; the auxiliary tank added 11gal more), which are easily recognizable by twin fuel inlets on the driver's side rear quarter panel. A valve under the driver's seat allowed the fuel pump to draw from either tank and a switch under the dash changed the fuel gauge reading to the tank currently in use.

Also available were: limited slip axles front and rear, free-wheeling front hubs, front or rear power takeoff, tow hooks and a winch; a skid plate to pro-

As the nineties began, the Bronco celebrated its 25th anniversary. Ford honored the venerable sport-utility's history with a Silver Anniversary model with special Currant Red paint, a custom interior, and anniversary badging. Ford Motor Company

tect the transfer case from stumps and rocks, higher sidewall 6.50x16 tires (7.35x15 tires were standard), a tachometer and custom instrument package, chrome bumpers and wheel covers, Mustang-style bucket seats (a bench seat was standard), padded dash, radio, heater, dual sun visors, emergency flashers, seatbelts, a dry air cleaner (an oil bath air cleaner was standard), 45- or 55-amp alternators, and 55- or 70-amp batteries. A heavy-duty suspension package could also be specified that increased the GVW from 3,800lb to 4,700lb.

Industry analysts projected that sales of 4x4 utility vehicles would reach 70,000 by 1970, an increase of 700 per-cent during the decade, and Ford expected the Bronco to capture a major share of that market. Actually, the Bronco *created* a market for comfortable 4x4 utility vehicles that it would soon share with Chevrolet's Blazer. The Bronco gave Ford a winning combination of economy or power (depending on whether a buyer specified the thrifty six or gutsy V-8), a comfortable ride, go-anywhere four-wheel-drive traction, and options galore. So even in the face of the larger, more luxurious Blazer from Chevrolet and the similarly designed Dodge Ramcharger, Ford kept the Bronco in its compact size with only minor styling changes through 1977. Along the way, upgrades such as disk front brakes and electronic ignition were made, but the market was changing.

Utility 4x4s had caught on with families as sure-footed transportation for those living in rural areas as well as recreation or multipurpose vehicles for those living in suburbia. In this setting, Chevrolet's Blazer—which shared sheet metal, drivetrain, and chassis components with Chevy's full-size pickups—began to pull ahead in sales. The production figure chart below tells the story.

Notice that at the start of the seventies, the Bronco held a lead on the Blazer, but by 1972 Blazer had not only pulled ahead but had *doubled* the Bronco's sales. Then notice how Bronco sales steadily fell while Blazer pulled ahead so that by the mid-seventies, Chevy was selling over *five times* as many copies of its 4x4 utility as Ford. These figures were obviously troubling to Ford management, which ordered development of a Bronco based on Ford's full-size pickup line. This totally new Bronco emerged in 1978. Bronco sales shot to 75,761 units that year, proving that Ford had again hit a winning combination.

The full-size Bronco's wheelbase grew to 104in with an overall length of 180in. Its width also increased to 79.3in. Powering this more substantial and heavier truck was Ford's 351ci V-8. In keeping with the market shift to commuting and recreational use, most were equipped with automatic transmissions. Color-keyed interiors and bucket seats

Sales of Chevrolet and Ford 4x4 Utility Vehicles

	1970	1971	1972	1973	1974	1975	1976
Blazer	11,527	17,220	44,266	44,821	56,728	50,548	74,389
Bronco	18,450	19,784	21,892	21,894	18,786	11,273	13,625

114

gave a more luxurious appearance that received full expression in the deluxe Ranger XLT. This upscale model hardly qualifies as a utility 4x4. It's better described as an all-wheel-drive boulevard cruiser. Stand-out features of the Ranger XLT included rectangular headlights, bright metal bumpers, a woodtone dash, deep pile carpet, tilt steering, and sliding side windows. With Bronco's sights set on the Blazer and not the jeep or Scout, a topless roadster no longer appeared in the lineup. The full-length metal top now formed an integral part of the body.

In 1980, the Bronco went on a slight diet, shrinking in overall length to 177.6in. With an eye toward fuel economy, Ford's 300ci six replaced the 351 V-8 as the base engine. The most significant change occurred in the front suspension, where Ford's Twin I Beam setup replaced the former rigid axle. The up-

grade to independent front suspension gave the Bronco a ride similar to that of a car, or at least nearly the ride of a Ford Twin I Beam pickup. Where the Bronco suffered in ride quality was the short wheelbase's tendency to buck and pitch on tar strips and uneven pavement.

Fickle is the best word to describe American car and truck buyers. By the mid-eighties, slim and trim had again become desirable qualities in a light truck or utility 4x4. In 1984 Ford met the market shift with its Bronco II, a look-alike but downsized version of the big Bronco using Ranger sheet metal and chassis elements. Ford aimed the slimmer, trimmer Bronco at Chevy's S-10 Blazer, and it proved to be a strong competitor. But there's another story here. The Bronco II's measurements match almost identically the original Bronco of 1966.

Ford added the Explorer to its truck line in 1991. The Explorer was created to replace the Bronco II, and was a more versatile vehicle since it was available with four passenger doors, not just two. It won Four-Wheeler magazine's Four-Wheeler of the Year award two years in a row, proving it was a vehicle that could perform as well as deliver a family car ride. Ford Motor Company

	1984 Bronco II	**Original Bronco**
Wheelbase	94in	92in
Overall length	158.4in	152.1in
Width	69.8in	68.8in
Height	68.2in	69.2in

So it goes to show, what's new ain't necessarily better, and it follows that original Broncos are popular with collectors.

Chapter 15

Ranchero:
Ford's Car/Pickup

Introduced November 12, 1956, at Quitman, Georgia, the Ranchero would stir emotions in many men's hearts. As it was offered, the Ranchero was a dream machine. It fast became the fashionable tow vehicle at the drag strips. Any respectable service station or body shop had one. When Petersen Publishing test-drove the first El Camino in 1959, it ran out of gas. The service station responded in a 1957 Ranchero.

The concept of basing a pickup on a company's car line was nothing new. The first pickups had been roadsters with carry-all boxes in place of the trunk. During the thirties, most light trucks shared styling and at least some sheet metal with their builder's car line. Hudson continued this approach on its pickups through the forties. The Ranchero's appeal is summed up in one word—versatility. It functioned as a light truck and yet escaped the social stigma associated with trucks of the time. Ads promoting the Ranchero's dual personality showed a gentlemen escorting his woman friend into a Ranchero at the end of an evening on the town.

Drawing as it did on what Ford's ads called its "Thunderbird Heritage," the Ranchero had class—something every other truck of the era, including the Chevy Cameo, lacked.

1957 Ranchero

The Ranchero used ball joint/coil spring front suspension from the Ford car line and was the only pickup in 1957 that did not have a solid front axle. In-

Ford completely changed the light truck market in 1957 with the introduction of its Ranchero. Now those who wanted a truck's utility but a car's comfort had a vehicle that offered both.

dependent front suspension gave this handsome pickup the driving and handling ease heretofore associated with a car. It led the rest of the pickup crowd in other ways as well. Ford made Select-Aire air conditioning an in-dash unit for 1957. Ranchero was the first light truck to offer such a feature. Ranchero brochures list the 223 six, 272 V-8, and 292 V-8 as the engine choices. Actual Ranchero patent plates reveal 312s, including dual quad and supercharged versions. A pickup so-equipped clearly wasn't intended as an around-town delivery wagon. Options such as automatic transmissions, power steering, power brakes, power seat, and power windows made the Ranchero the "Continental" of the commercial vehicles.

The lines on Ford's all-new 1957 car line emphasized length. Forward angled front fenders form a wide brow over the protruding single headlamp. (Quad headlamps were planned but hadn't yet been approved by all forty-eight states.) A crease, starting at the headlight, angled down over the front wheel arch. A similar arch outlined the rear wheel cutouts. Tail fins, that familiar fifties styling feature, began just behind the door handle, canted slightly outward as they reached the end of the pickup box, and formed a spear at the top of the jettube taillamps shared by all Fords, including T-Bird.

Interior schemes for the standard Ranchero (model 66A) combined tan and brown Sharkskin Woven-Plastic with tan Crush-Grain vinyl bolsters or blue French-Stitch vinyl on cushions and seatbacks with white Crush-Grain vinyl bolsters. The door panels match those of the Del Rio Ranch Wagon model 59B. The Sof-Tread floor covering looks like carpet but cleans like linoleum.

The cargo area would always be Ranchero's strong point. For 1957 a Ranchero could handle a payload of up to 1,190lb for a maximum GVW of 4,600lb. Since the tailgate lowers flush with the cargo floor, the 6ft floor area extends to nearly 8ft with the tailgate down.

1958 Ranchero

Speculation by most automobile writers had been that Chevrolet and Plymouth would introduce their versions of the Ranchero for 1958. This wasn't so. Of all the new Ford models, Ranchero wore the revised frontal styling best. Quad headlamps were now legal and appeared on all Ford cars and trucks. Custom series Rancheros (66B) matched Custom 300 car trim. All 66B models had the gold insert side spear whether style-toned, two-toned, or monotoned.

The most noted feature of the 1958 Ranchero is its use of the 1957 taillights and tailgate. Since the 1958 wagons got the taillight restyle, why not the Ranchero? The reason has to do with the Courier, not the Ranchero. On the Courier, station wagon tailgate components were bolted together to form a liftgate, so there was no way to run the wiring to use the new tailgate-mounted lights. Since both the Ranchero and the Courier were commercial offerings, the Ranchero also got the carryover tailgate and rear lights. Anyone who has owned a 1958 Ford wagon can tell you how easy it is to break the tailgate-mounted lights when loading or hauling with the tailgate in the down position. The use of the 1957 taillights is obviously a blessing in a work vehicle like a Ranchero. From the

In 1957, Ford unveiled its dazzling Ranchero. To create this car/pickup, Ford stylists cut the top off the cargo section of a two-door station wagon. Rancheros weren't heavy haulers, but what they lacked in load capacity they more than made up for in looks. This example is owned by Greg Plonski.

The Ranchero borrowed many body stampings from the Del Rio and Ranch Wagon to keep tooling costs to a minimum. In fact, so much of the Ranchero's body structure is derived from a station wagon that removing the cargo floor of a Ranchero reveals a station wagon floor pan. Early production versions suffered from water leaking into this wagon understructure. The Ranchero also shared the wagon's tailgate and a bumper common to all Custom Series cars and wagons. The tailgate handle, also from the wagon, covered the hole for the wagon's lock cylinder with the Ranchero emblem. A body-colored molding (or bright molding on deluxe 66B) outlined the top of the tailgate and bed and continued up the cab's rear pillar, where it went across the back of the roof. All Ranchero models had bright windshield and rear backlight reveal moldings plus bright framed vent windows.

With the wraparound windshield (a styling must for the era), instrument panel glare from the sun was a big problem. Ford solved this with an overhang that acted as a visor above the instruments. The steering wheel, like the instrument panel, was of Ford's LifeGuard Safety Design. The deep-dished wheel had the Ford crest in its center, while the patterned outer edge of the horn hub carried Ford Master Guide Power Steering lettering on Rancheros so optioned.

For 1957, Rancheros were offered in two trim lines: Standard and Custom. The Standard Ranchero, shown here, used the Custom series side trim and small hubcaps. The Custom Ranchero used the Custom 300 series trim and full disk, turbine-style, wheel covers.

Sedan deliveries of the forties and fifties are also popular with collectors. Like the Ranchero, Ford's sedan deliveries began with *a two-door station wagon. This 1958 example is owned by Jack Lewis.*

Several Edsel collectors have created a Ranchero that never was by grafting on an Edsel *front clip and side trim. The result is a very unusual pickup.*

rear, you can distinguish between a 1957 and 1958 Ranchero by looking at the bumper guards.

The new 300hp Interceptor 352 Special V-8, fitted with a four-barrel carburetor and requiring premium fuel, topped the engine list. In production, some Rancheros were equipped with the new 332, as well as carryover 312 V-8. The 332 came in 240hp and 265hp versions. Data plate numbers have revealed these unlisted engine options.

Starting in 1955, Ford began offering carpet kits for models not having carpet as standard equipment. The carpet was shipped with the vehicle as wheel covers are and installed at the dealership before delivery. Therefore, carpeting in 1957-1958 Rancheros and Couriers is correct. Another option that may have been adaptable for Rancheros and Couriers was FordAire suspension (originally intended for the Fairlane series and wagons). The Ranchero's wagon frame made this option possible. Few Fords received this option and maybe not even one Ranchero or Courier. However, there is always the possibility.

1959 Ranchero

Compared to its competition, namely Chevrolet and Plymouth, Ford's styling for 1959 was fresh but conservative. In this last year for wraparound windshields, the glass curved farther into the roof. Many of the styling touches reflected "jet age" influence. Parking lamps, now located in the pods at the ends of the front bumper, resembled jet engine intakes. At the rear, the large round taillamps sat in turbine-finned bezels. For 1959, Ford placed its entire car line on one wheelbase. This increased the Ranchero's length by 2in, resulting in a longer cargo box. Only one Ranchero model is listed, the Custom.

1960-1965 Falcon Ranchero

By chassis platform and body styling, Rancheros fall into four basic groups. The original 1957-1959 models were derived from full-size Fords. The second group, 1960-1965, consisted of Falcon-based Ranchero compacts. The third, 1966-1971, were Fairlane-based (the 1966 Ranchero used a Fairlane body with a Falcon front), while the fourth, the 1972-1979 models, used the Gran Torino/LTD II body shell. Of these four groups, the most overlooked is the Fal-

con Rancheros. Yet all the Falcon Rancheros are handsome vehicles.

January 1960 saw the introduction of the new Ranchero derived from the Falcon two-door station wagon. This was a very handsome, low-cost work vehicle. Yes, the downsized Ranchero could still work and had a payload capacity of 800lb. By comparison, the 1960 El Camino (which was based on the full-size Chevrolet) could only handle 700lb, and it didn't really handle even that much weight very well. During Ranchero's first three years it had been America's most luxurious pickup. Now it was America's lowest priced pickup.

In downsizing to a compact, the Ranchero's wheelbase shrank 9 1/2in,

but the cargo bed was still 6ft (72in) long. The bed's 31.6 cubic feet of cargo space was easy to load with a floor height of just 27in and side-loading height of only 38.9in. The trim 189in-long Falcon Ranchero used an all-steel, welded unit-body construction, which gave it maximum rigidity with minimum weight.

The Falcon 144.3ci six put out 90hp and sipped regular gas. Buyers could choose between a manual three-speed transmission or optional Ford-O-Matic. With gas mileage approaching an honest 30mpg, the Falcon Ranchero was very economical to operate. Inside, standard trim consisted of brown, western-motif vinyl with beige bolsters. Dual sun vi-

Ford created the Ranchero by removing the rear roof section from its two-door station wagon and installing a cargo bed in the rear seat area—giving a 6ft load space, or nearly 8ft. with the tailgate lowered.

sors and armrests, a dome light, rearview mirror, spare tire and wheel (stored behind the seat), dispatch box, ash tray, and foam rubber seat padding were all standard features. Deluxe interior trim was available in black-and-white or red-and-white vinyl. A white steering wheel with full trim ring came as part of this option. The wide cab provided adequate space for three adults.

On the outside, the compact Ranchero received its good looks from the Fal-

121

The Ranchero's interior reflected the color styling of Ford's new car line. The "dished" steering wheel design offered the driver a margin of safety in a collision and seat belts (not shown) were also offered, as an option. The 1957 Ranchero shown in these and accompanying photos is owned by Ron Fisher of Indianapolis, Indiana.

con's well-sculpted lines. A bright metal grille, chrome bumpers and windshield, and back-light trim were all standard. A deluxe trim package added bright metal cargo bed trim. Full wheel covers and white sidewalls were also available. The Ranchero's small size and simple styling were the look America wanted, as is evi-

denced by sales averaging 20,000 units a year for the compact Ranchero's six-year production run.

While outwardly the 1961 Ranchero received only a new convex, as opposed to concave, grille, for 1962 the Falcon Ranchero got a more substantial facelift. The addition of a Thunderbird-inspired hood scoop gave the frontal styling a bolder appearance. Round taillamps, which were becoming a Ford styling trademark, would be used through 1965.

Plans had called for the Ranchero to leave the Falcon line in 1963 due to the lack of a V-8. The Fairlane intermediate line was growing and was expected to include a two-door station wagon that

would serve as a platform for both a sedan delivery and Ranchero. Instead, Ford decided to share Fairlane suspension and driveline components on the Falcon, so the Ranchero stayed in the Falcon line and got its V-8.

For 1964 the Falcon saw its first major styling update, receiving more angular lines that would mark Ford's look for the mid-sixties. The new sheet metal and expanded interior space carried over for 1965, Ranchero's last year as a "compact." Competition in the form of a new intermediate-size El Camino, based on the Chevelle, had debuted the year before, and some at Ford regretted not switching the Falcon to the Fairlane line earlier to make it more competitive. Still, the Ranchero had a lot to offer. Four model choices were now available: model 66A (standard), 66B (deluxe), 66G, and 66H. The 66G was also a standard model, but with bucket seats. Only sixteen of these were built, making them extremely rare. The deluxe 66H also had buckets and 990 copies of this model were sold. The deluxe Rancheros wore a narrow, full-length trim strip taken from the 1964 Falcon Futura.

Durango: Ford's Last "Ranchero"
by Gene Makrancy

The Ford Motor Company quickly realized that dropping the Ranchero in 1979 was a mistake. There was a demand for car/pickups in several regions. With the energy situation at that time, the Falcon Ranchero formula that had worked in 1960 would be the way to go. The Fairmont was the current "compact" at Ford. Money was tightening and Ranchero prototypes based on the new full-size LTD were stillborn. Funding battles were being fought between car and truck divisions, so an outside firm was chosen to provide a solution that was named the Durango.

National Coach Corporation, associated with Econoline chassis and cut-away conversions, took on the task. The Futura with its unique coupe style lent itself to the modification. Simplicity of the conversion was its high point. The FRP (fiberglass reinforced plastic) bed fastened in cuts made in the existing body lines and moldings hid it all. No paint work was done following the conversion, although steel was welded in at some cuts for more structural safety.

Quarter panel extensions were replaced with units that housed spring-loaded hinge supports for the tailgate that wore Futura taillamps. Hardware was cadmium plated and used Ford parts bin steel cables. The inside tailgate handle was a Ford item, too. Even the three Durango nameplates were designed to pop into holes where the Futura emblem was removed.

The Durango could be optioned with all applicable Fairmont Futura accessories and options, with unique items such as a tonneau cover, fiberglass canopy shell, air-adjustable shocks, cargo bed liner, center console, deluxe bucket seats, rear-opening window, custom wheels and tires, cargo tiedowns, and cargo side rails. A GT version with TRX suspension and engine performance was planned but never built.

Things were bad now at Ford, and white collar workers were being let go. National reported that approximately 120-211 Durango units were produced. This is a far cry from the 12,000-20,000 units a year National had been promised by Ford. Some were based on the Mercury Z-7. Production spanned the 1981 and 1982 model years. All Durangos that were built were sold, and

they inevitably draw crowds when they turn up at shows. Ford made the same mistake with the Durango that Hudson had made with the Italia, which was a unique car that they forgot to tell their dealers about. There is little doubt that the Durango would have been a bigger success if had not been such a secret.

Gene Makrancy is president of the Ranchero Club, Ranchero devotee without equal, and the expert on these notable pickup/cars.

Unquestionably the most unusual, lowest production Ford pickup is the Durango—a custom job created from the Ford Futura by National Coach Corporation. Initial plans had been for the Durango to have a fairly high production run, but the project died with only a few hundred units made.

1966-1971 Fairlane Ranchero

The restyled Falcon carried the long hood, short deck design inspired by the very successful Mustang. The long hood also worked well on the Ranchero, which had grown nearly a foot in overall length. This added length benefited the cargo area, which could now hold objects up to 6 1/2ft (78in) long with the tailgate closed. The new styling had a less boxy appearance, achieved by rounding the leading edge of the front fenders and hood and letting the line from the windshield pillars curve gracefully over the top of the cab. The "kick-up" rear quarter panel styling, borrowed from the Mustang, helped break the slab-sided look of the earlier models. The cab now afforded enough room to store the spare tire and jack behind the seat on the passenger side, with space on the driver's side for a small suitcase or other items. Curved side windows, combined with a 3in increase in overall width, afforded more shoulder and seat room.

In 1967, Ford completed the transition of moving the Ranchero from the Falcon to the Fairlane line. A Fairlane grille with stacked headlights was added, and the Ranchero received Fairlane nameplates. But other than these changes, the body shell and basic design remained the same. In keeping with Ford's two-year styling cycle, a more significant facelift would occur in 1968.

From 1957-1965, the Ranchero had shared front doors with the two-door station wagon and sedan delivery. In 1966, with the elimination of both the sedan delivery and two-door wagon, the Ranchero doors had to be modified from sedan doors with a special framing structure for the glass and vent windows. For 1968, Ford designers eliminated that window framing structure in a clever cost-cutting move that gave the Ranchero a "hardtop" appearance. A wide grille, set between forward thrusting tips of the front fenders, lent a strong Thunderbird styling influence. Other distinctions of this model year include the side marker lights, required by the federal government, and fender crest that now ran straight from the front to the back of the vehicle, creating an impression of lowness and added length.

With 1969 falling as the second year of Ford's two-year styling cycle, the Ranchero remained virtually unchanged. The most prominent new feature is a hood scoop that's about as subtle as Cyrano De Bergerac's famous nose. By the late sixties, upscale was the way to go, and besides the standard Ranchero, Ford also offered a Ranchero 500 and GT. Upscale appointments found in these deluxe models include deep pile carpeting and fancier seat and door coverings. The deluxe models are easily recognized by added bright metal trim and Ranchero 500 or GT badges.

The final styling cycle for this body shell gave the 1970 and 1971 Rancheros a mild version of the "Coke bottle" or

---

The Finale: The Limited Production Ranchero
by Gene Makrancy

The 1979 model year would see the last Ranchero. In addition to the Ranchero, the highly successful intermediate platform begun in 1972 was being laid to rest. This platform included the Gran Torino, Montego, LT-DII, Cougar, XR-7, Elite, Thunderbird, Mark IV, and Mark V. The demise of all these specialty cars left Ford with a great pool of parts, accessories, performance, and luxury items. Wait and see where they showed up.

Ford not only pioneered the pickup/car format in 1957 with the first Ranchero, but it also pioneered pickup luxury. The 1957 Ranchero was the first pickup truck with in-dash air conditioning, power windows, power seats, and a number of other luxury items. For the last Ranchero Ford planned a special farewell edition that would top them all.

The 1979 1/2 Limited Production Ranchero was the most luxurious pickup produced to date—and it may never be outdone. The first impressive feature of this car/pickup is its length, over 220in. Although the hood seems almost as long as the box, the cargo area measured 6 3/4ft (80in) long with 49in between the wheelwells. Standard load rating was over a half-ton with some equipped and titled as three-quarter-tonners. (Work capability is a luxury, not standard in pickup/cars.)

Of its many special features, the Limited Production Ranchero's strong point is its interior. Here is where this vehicle becomes unique. The dash pad is genuine hand-sewn leather, as is the steering wheel wrap. Full instrumentation is complemented by full accessories, including a lights-on warning system, air conditioning, intermittent wipers, AM/FM stereo (quadrasonic eight-track or cassette available), tilt wheel, cruise control, and rich burled walnut appliqués. Seating consists of real leather-covered, twin comfort lounge seats with six-way power adjustment. Door trim panels are from the Cougar XR-7 with full length arm rests and control pods for power windows, power door locks, remote control mirrors, and an ashtray. Thick carpeting covers the floor and additional sound deadening materials were used throughout.

All Limited Production Rancheros feature dark red interior coloring. The four exterior color choices were dark red, white, dove gray, or silver. A special order of 116 Rancheros painted 2J Maroon were built for the Houston office, but records do not show if these were Limited Production models. However, one 2J Maroon Ranchero was built in Lorain, Ohio, and it is an LP. I know, because it's mine! All Limited Productions are fitted with vinyl tops in white, dark red, or maroon. Wire wheel covers could be exchanged for Magnum 500s or the 15in turbine-style aluminum wheels. In other respects, an LP looks like a standard Ranchero from the outside. Because of this, some district offices complained that the truck was too plain on the outside to justify the price. So a test unit was modified using Thunderbird/Cougar XR-7 trim. The longer wheelbase and bigger rear wheel opening of the pickup/car required that some of the trim be specially manufactured. Only one Ranchero was so equipped, and that's my Ranchero. Besides the maroon paint and maroon vinyl top, it has maroon vinyl insert side moldings, maroon bumper guards and rub strips, maroon taillight bezel accents, maroon accents to the turbine rims, and a maroon accent on the complimentary gold owner initial plaques. The background color on the hood ornament is also maroon.

Besides the special trim, my LP has rocker panel trim and extensions, cornering lamps, hood accent moldings, rear mount power antenna, wheel locks, spare tire lock, locking gas cap, door edge guards, and carpeted floor mats. Interior goodies continue with dual illuminated visor mirrors and the courtesy light group that consists of door panel lights, underdash lights, back panel lights, and an interior cargo light. An automatic seat belt release affords easy access to the cavernous interior cargo space that stretches from the back of the seat to the rear axle area. This space is upholstered and can be hidden by color-keyed flaps and the spare tire cover. Even the glove box is lined and contained a thank-you card for purchasing a Limited Production Ranchero.

These luxurious pickup/cars sold in such small numbers probably because they came with a price tag that was $800 over the base price of a 1979 Lincoln sedan.

pinched midsection look that GM stylists applied quite successfully to that company's late-sixties muscle cars and intermediates. On the Ranchero, the front bumper now wrapped around the leading edge of the front fenders, and the obtrusive hood scoop had disappeared. For owners of country estates, or those who would like to give this impression, a new upscale Squire model carried simulated wood paneling on the sides of the body and tailgate. Distinctive Squire interior features included a wood appliqué panel under the instruments and a simulated wood inlay in the steering wheel. During this period it was Ford's custom to market limited edition "Spring Specials." With Ranchero, these appeared in the 500 and GT lines and are identified by boldly colored side stripes plus brightly colored interiors.

1972-1979 Gran Torino/ LTD Ranchero

In 1957, Ford's full-size Ranchero rode on a 116in wheelbase. In 1972, the Ranchero, now in the Torino intermediate line, had a 118in wheelbase. So extensive was the new engineering and styling that only the engines carried over. Besides added length, the Ranchero also got a full perimeter frame (while in the Falcon/Fairlane lines, the Ranchero's construction had been unit-body). A dramatic sheet metal transformation marked by a hood that appeared almost as long as the box combined with an aggressive, oval-shape grille opening to emphasize the Ranchero's power image. High output engines, including a RamAir 429 rated at 215hp, brought the power image to life.

In many ways 1973 served as a transitional year. Styling changes consisted mainly of a widened grille and flattened hood. Yet 1973 would prove to be Ranchero's most popular year with 45,741 units built. Probably the most significant change appeared in the form of federally mandated 5mph impact-absorbing bumpers. Critics called them chrome railroad ties, but Ranchero wore the new bumper better than the passenger cars.

A grille restyle again marked the 1974 models. The Ranchero's appearance would remain unchanged through 1976, but that doesn't mean Ford left its car/pickup alone for these three model years. The 250 six came out of the engine line-up early in 1974, making the 302 V-8 the base engine for most of that year. For 1975, engine options dropped in number from six to three, with the standard engine now a 351 two-barrel V-8, rated at an anemic 145hp. The seventies saw auto manufacturers wrestling to meet increasingly stringent federal emissions standards, and the result turned engines that had been muscular Goliaths into fuel-guzzling wimps. Just as the impact-absorbing bumpers had made styling waves in 1973, catalytic converters brought cat calls and hisses for 1975. Along with the converters, the fuel tank had a slimmer inlet to fit the new nozzles on the unleaded gasoline pumps. A decal placed over the filler cap warned owners not to use leaded fuel.

The Ranchero's last styling change, given in 1977, would hold through to the end of production in 1979. Ford had moved the Ranchero into the LTD line where squared-off lines prevailed, so changes for 1977 would flatten the sen-

In 1960, Ford downsized the Ranchero to its new compact Falcon platform. In the process the car/pickup's wheelbase shrank 9 1/2in but the designers managed to maintain the larger pickup's load length of 6 1/2ft. Ford advertised its new Falcon Ranchero as the lowest cost pickup in America. The example seen here is a 1965 model.

suous curves that had made the 1972-1976 models so appealing. The 302 V-8 reappeared as the base engine. Rancheros from the three final years are virtual look-alikes.

Probably the most noteworthy comment that can be made of these end-of-the-line Rancheros is the extreme low volume of the wood-paneled Squire, which dropped from 1,126 in 1977 to 907 in 1978 and to an almost custom-built level of 758 for 1979. By 1980, declining sales were driving the number two auto maker into a collision course with disaster. In this setting, the Ranchero, which had revolutionized pickup styling, ride, handling, and performance, quietly disappeared. There would be one more car/pickup to carry the Ford name, but it wouldn't be built by Ford.

Appendices

Looking into the Hobby

If you have recently purchased a vintage Ford pickup, you're likely to have questions about sources or parts, or you may want to contact others who own similar trucks. The club listings that follow will link you with others who share your interest in vintage Ford trucks. The book listings give you sources of historical and other information to aid you in purchasing or restoring a collectible Ford pickup.

Clubs/Publications

Early Ford V-8 Club of America
P.O. Box 2122
San Leandro, CA 94577
This international club supports the preservation of all early V-8 Fords, including pickups.

ECON-O
The Econoline Organization
15039 Costela St.
San Leandro, CA 945790
This club is a nationwide organization of owners of 1961-1967 Ford Econoline and Falcon vans and pickups. It publishes a semiregular newsletter with technical, mechanical, and parts articles, letters, and free classified ads for Econoline-related items.

Model A Ford Club of America
250 S. Cypress
LaHabra, CA 90631

Model A Restorers Club
24822 Michigan Ave.
Dearborn, MI 48121
These international clubs support the preservation of Model A Fords of all types, including pickups and larger trucks.

Model T Ford Club of America
41 Reeland Ave.
Warwick, RI 02886

Model T Ford Club International
P.O. Box 438315
Chicago, IL 60643
These international clubs support the preservation of Model T Fords of all types, including pickups and larger trucks. Both clubs offer magazine-quality bimonthly publications, hold national meets, and have regional chapters.

F-100 Supernationals
c/o Pat Ford Promotions
1920 Council Ave.
Statesville, NC 28677
This is not a club. It is the world's largest gathering of Ford pickups, held annually at Pigeon Forge, Tennessee. The F-100 Supernationals is a family-oriented gathering of trucks and parts vendors,

with tech workshops, show competition, parades, and related events.

'49-50-51 Ford Owners Newsletter
1733 S. Willow Dr.
Midwest City, OK 73130
Although not a club per se, this publication conducts many club functions including an annual national meet. Benefits to Ford truck owners include a column in the newsletter on Ford trucks and occasional publication of Ford truck service bulletins.

The Ranchero Club
1339 Beverly Road
Port Vue, PA 15133
This club is the final authority on Rancheros. It publishes a bimonthly newsletter and cooperates with various shows and events.

This Old Truck
Box 838
Yellow Springs, OH 45387
This bimonthly publication covers all makes of light trucks, including Ford, and provides technical assistance to owners of vintage trucks.

Literature—Books

Catalog of Ford Truck ID Numbers 1946-72 by the staff of *Cars & Parts* magazine

Translates Ford truck VIN numbers, color codes, trim codes, and transmission codes. A very useful book for determining a truck's origins and original equipment.

Ford Pickups 1932-52 by Mack Hils

Excellent photo coverage of Ford pickups of this period. Available from Mack Products, Moberly, Missouri.

How to Restore Your Ford Pickup by Tom Brownell

Complete restoration guidelines and instructions for all years of Ford pickups. Available from Classic Motorbooks.

Illustrated Ford Pickup Buyer's Guide by Paul G. McLaughlin

A year-by-year look at Ford light trucks with value and appreciation ratings. Available from Classic Motorbooks.

Ford Pickup Repair: Pickups of the '70s.

Contains reprints of *Hot Rod Magazine* articles on performance-tuning Ford F-series two-wheel-drive trucks of seventies vintage. Available from Classic Motorbooks.

Ford Pickup Trucks 1948-56, Development History and Restoration Guide by Paul G. McLaughlin

Excellent historical coverage of Ford trucks of this period. Contains reprints of original ads and very helpful lists of specifications. Available from Classic Motorbooks.

Ford Pickups 1957-67: How to Identify, Select, and Restore Ford Collector Light-Trucks, Panels, and Rancheros by Paul G. McLaughlin

Excellent historical coverage of Ford trucks of this period. Contains photos, ad reprints, and helpful lists of specifica-tions. Available from Classic Motorbooks.

Heavyweight Book of American Light - Duty Trucks 1939-1966 by Tom Brownell and Don Bunn

Comprehensive coverage of all American light trucks of this period; contains restoration information on renewing hydraulic brakes, replacing wiring, and rebuilding a straight-axle front end. Available from Classic Motorbooks.

How to Restore Your Collector Car by Tom Brownell

Step-by-step presentation of procedures for restoring a car or light truck. Topics include stripping, derusting, metal repair, priming, painting, security measures to prevent theft, preparing for show competition, and more. Available from Classic Motorbooks.

Index